I0802051

Challenges and Choices

Discovering the Proper Use of Agency

Challenges and Choices

Discovering the Proper Use of Agency

Alan Mangum

CFI
Springville, Utah

ISBN 13: 978-1-59955-095-4

Published by CFI, an imprint of Cedar Fort, Inc., 2373 W. 700 S., Springville, UT, 84663
Distributed by Cedar Fort, Inc., www.cedarfort.com

LIBRARY OF CONGRESS CATALOGING-IN-PUBLICATION DATA

Mangum, Alan, 1956–
Challenges and Choices / Alan Mangum.
p. cm.
ISBN 978-1-59955-095-4
1. Christian life—Mormon authors. I. Title.

BX8656.M345 2007
248.4'893—dc22

2007032014

Cover design by Nicole Williams
Cover design © 2007 by Lyle Mortimer

Printed in the United States of America

10 9 8 7 6 5 4 3 2 1

Printed on acid-free paper

Dedication

To my children—may you always know of my unconditional love, and of my willingness to provide as much assistance as is appropriate along whatever path you choose. I am proud of your amazing progress and where you each are now, and I look forward to your continued safety and success. May God bless and protect you along the way.

And to my beloved Linda—you have always been my reason to keep going when even I didn't know if I could, and I admire you so for your willingness to hang in there even when you thought you couldn't. Through it all we have always turned to each other—and to God—and that has made all the difference. There are not words enough to express the depth of my love and of my desire to be worthy of you.

Table of Contents

Foreword

Having been asked by the author to write the foreword for *Challenges and Choices*, I feel a tremendous responsibility to say something that will encourage you to read and digest this writing, because we all have challenges in our lives, and the choices we make in resolving these challenges can, and will, make a difference in our future. Someone once said that the decisions we make in life will have eternal consequences. Think about this as you contemplate the myriad decisions you make each day. Then know that this book is an inspirational gift, a must for every reader, to assist them in making choices that will bless them and their families for eternity.

A little background might be helpful. I first met Alan Mangum when he was a young missionary for The Church of Jesus Christ of Latter-day Saints while I served as president of the mission he was sent to labor in. He was a great missionary with unusual strengths who developed a thorough understanding of the gospel. I watched him develop the talents the Lord had blessed him with. He has served in many callings in the Church since his full-time mission, but he has especially thrived in his many callings as a teacher of the gospel. Readers will recognize his knowledge and understanding of the scriptures as they read the inspirational pages of this book.

Alan's marriage to Linda was a blessing to both, and they have grown together as a couple through the experiences they have faced together. They have been blessed with four children and felt the same excitement at their children's births as any parents do. With every hope and desire, they did all they could to teach their children correct principles, but as the years went on, each of their children became involved in things that were totally contrary to what they had been taught by parents, Church leaders, and others. Because of these challenges, their family had many hard choices to make. I'm sure this sounds familiar to every reader.

Through their challenges Alan's family learned to depend on the Lord, and instead of letting those challenges drive them apart, they have come together in a remarkable way. This has been a great blessing to them as well as to their children.

I was privileged to read various drafts of this manuscript as Alan prepared it for publication. As I pondered his words as he was writing this book, the gospel principles that he used, and the ways he and his family went about resolving their challenges, I realized that this was a book everyone should read and ponder. Let me just say that because of proper choices, prayer and fasting, plus an outpouring of love, things in the author's family have changed greatly for the better.

As I read this book, I asked myself, *How would I have handled that challenge?* I will be honest and say that if I had been wise, I would have handled it the same way they did. Their success in facing some of the most difficult challenges parents can face is inspirational and motivating.

The principles of the gospel of Jesus Christ are found throughout this book. As I read it, I found it hard to put down, and I can only say I'm a better husband, father, and grandfather for having had this experience. I would like to thank my dear friend, Alan Mangum, for teaching me so well and being an inspiration in my life.

Jack H. Goaslind
Emeritus General Authority

Acknowledgments

It's a daunting experience to sit in front of a blank computer screen with the intent of writing a book. It's even more daunting to take a rough draft of the first chapter to a former General Authority, to a former bishop and stake president who also happens to have taught in the Seminary and Institute program for over thirty years, and to a close personal friend who is one of the most critical readers and thinkers I will ever know, and ask for their opinions of my effort. That their responses were, and have continued to be, so overwhelmingly positive has not only made it possible for me to continue with the process, but has also helped me to gain the confidence necessary to trust my own thoughts and feelings about how to best present this material.

So to Elder Jack H. Goaslind, Greg Downs, and Jared Shaver, I can only say that I couldn't have done it without you. None of you can ever know how much your support has helped in the process, and none of you will ever acknowledge the untold contributions that you have each made.

To Craig Ramsey, my friend of so many years now, I couldn't have done it without your help either. Your assistance in clarifying my approach to the psychological concepts of Principle Three made it possible for me to complete the most difficult part of the entire book. I truly could never have finished it without your support and insight into what I was really trying to say.

A simple thank you isn't enough, and so I say to you all, Brethren, I salute you.

To Vern Utley, Jim Smith, Denise Pacheco, and the entire staff at Life-Line—thank you for saving another life, and for all the additional perspective you have added to our thinking and approach to some of life's most difficult challenges.

To Lyle Mortimer and the staff at Cedar Fort, I will never be able to adequately express my gratitude for your willingness to take a chance on what is a difficult, but critically important, subject. And to Lyndsee Cordes, thank you for your patience and expertise in smoothing out the rough spots and *really* getting things ready for publication. From the bottom of my heart, thank you for your combined efforts on behalf of this book.

Finally, I must express the love and gratitude that I have for my family members and the friends whose experiences have also been used as examples to add so much to the overall message. That they would place so much trust in my ability to tell our joint stories in a way that could be helpful to others, while also maintaining their dignity and privacy, says far more about them than it does about me.

Beloved Linda, dearest family and friends, I am humbled beyond words and am forever in your debt.

Introduction

As human beings, we are endowed with freedom of choice, and we cannot shuffle off our responsibility upon the shoulders of God or nature. We must shoulder it ourselves. It is up to us.

A. J. Toynbee, British historian and Christian apologist

Oh the challenges and choices of life and the learning experiences that they bring with them, especially the really tough ones.

So just what is your toughest challenge? What is it that brings you to these pages in the first place? Does your toughest challenge revolve around you yourself, a child or spouse, drugs or drink, pornography or philandering, physical or mental illness, abuse—or any of an innumerable list of others?

Or, as is the case for most of us, is it some combination of these?

But the real challenge isn't what someone else does to or around you, or even what you do to yourself. What matters more than anything else in this world is how *you choose* to deal with those challenges. Which can only mean that everything contained here is simply about your absolute right to choose the course of your life, and the absolute accountability this requires of you.

What qualifies me to write such a book? What do I know about tough challenges and how to deal with them? Not much when compared to some people's experiences, but quite a bit more than I did about nine years ago when my wife and I were forced to begin dealing with some very tough challenges as the result of some choices our children have made.

How tough has it been, you ask?

Tough enough that we have had major challenges with all four of our children, challenges so significant that three of them will fight the battle with drug addiction every day for the rest of their lives. Which means that over the last nine years we have been confronted with many, if not most, of the challenges that can befall young people in this day and age. Which also means that we are intimately familiar with the fear, heartache, and pain that come from watching our precious children make ever more dangerous and damaging choices. We are firsthand witnesses to the loss of self-esteem, the decrease in ability to reason clearly, and the seeming loss of ability to even make a choice—any choice—caused by the insidious enslavement of drugs and their destructive effects.

We have also witnessed the miracle of the positive changes that have come about in their lives in recent years too. Not that they are ready for Church activity, because, as of this writing, none of our children are active in any church or seem to have any interest in becoming churchgoers any time in the near future. But when you have been to the awful places that we have there is a time when, as important as it is, their church participation must take a backseat to the far more pressing matters of survival, sobriety, positive experiences in a day-to-day existence, and the opportunity for a long life without the horrors of drugs and the enslavement that they bring. There is no question that the effects of the Spirit of God are paramount in helping to throw off the chains of addiction, but just because someone develops a personal and healing relationship with God does not mean that they are ready for participation in any church activities.

All things in good time—and in God's time.

But this book cannot just be about what our children have done, for such a book would either be far too boring or far too frightening to be of much value. We will instead focus on the combination of basic doctrine and basic thinking that have made it possible for my wife and me to survive these very grueling challenges—survive not only with our marriage intact and wonderfully healthy, but also with a generally warm and loving association with our children. We will also spend more time talking about the practical application of gospel principles than we will defining them. Not that there isn't doctrinal exposition here, just that it is not the primary focus of the book.

In addition, the gospel teaching I have done over many years has only reinforced in my heart the fact that very few of us understand the enormous significance of the phrase, "The power is in them wherein they are agents unto themselves" (D&C 58:28). This is the concept of basic agency and, as previously stated, the absolute right that you have to determine the course of your own life.

So, if you decide you want to take this journey, you need to be prepared to make a detailed examination of your own thoughts, feelings, attitudes, and behaviors.

Why such an in-depth examination of your thinking?

Because it is that current thinking that leads to your personal behavior in all respects, and it also leads to your reactions to the behavior of those around you. Simply because "the power is within you" to change that thinking, and to thereby change the course of your life.

Which means that even if you already have a reasonable understanding of the doctrine of agency and the personal power that it grants you, it is almost guaranteed that you will find something here that either directly challenges that understanding, or directly points a finger of responsibility at you for something that you may not have considered before or that you might not want to consider now.

It is important for you to know that I am not a licensed mental health professional and that I do not have any kind of degree in psychiatry, psychology, or social work. What I do have is an almost lifelong interest in how we think and how those thoughts then make us who we are. It is an interest that goes back nearly forty years now, and as a result I have spent almost as much time studying different approaches to counseling and personal change as I have studying the scriptures. Not that that means anything in and of itself; I mention it simply to establish the fact that I have a more than passing familiarity with some of the most potent and frequently used treatment modalities in the world of mental health.

At the same time, all of the information that addresses specific psychological principles has been reviewed extensively by a licensed mental health professional.

This book is divided into six main principles and has a series of chapters under each of those headings. Principles One and Two will establish the doctrinal foundation that is required for the rest of the book to have any real meaning. Principle Three deals with the specifics of how we think and the importance of our attitudes about what we think, and it gives a very brief overview of some basic approaches to changing our thinking. Principle Four addresses the effects of our thinking and behaviors, both from the spiritual and physical standpoints. Principle Five presents some of the basic parenting concepts that have been both used and learned to help us cope with everything. This section also gives the most specific examples contained here about how those principles have been applied in our home.

All of which brings us to Principle Six, which is the real point of the whole book. For this is the principle that details the only real solution to any of our problems or trials: even the Lord Jesus Christ.

It is also important to note that the book is designed based on progressive thinking, so please fight the temptation to read ahead. Try to follow them in order the first time through.

Finally, it must be stated that I alone am responsible for everything contained here. As a regular Church member without any form of official sanction or responsibility, it can be no other way. Thus, everything that follows is based on my own understanding and experience and must not be interpreted as official Church doctrine or position on any of the issues addressed here.

And if you are still interested after all of that, there just might be something here that can help you with whatever your challenges are.

So let's begin . . .

Principle One

"Behold, Here Is the Agency of Man"

(D&C 93:31)

1.1 Laying Foundations

A WELL-KNOWN PROVERB USUALLY ATTRIBUTED to the Chinese simply says, "May you live in interesting times"—both a blessing and a curse. This appears to be an appropriate place for us to begin our discussion together.

It seems to me that anyone who does not recognize that we are living in interesting times simply isn't paying attention, for surely these are the most interesting times in all the long history of the world. In the short fifty years of my life we have gone from black-and-white TVs and party-line telephones to flat-screen HDTVs with theatre-quality sound and phone calls that take place solely in the unregulated world of the Internet. We have moved from a world where polio and small pox were among of the most feared of diseases to a world where those and many others that were greatly feared have been eradicated, and we are now able to examine the DNA molecules that determine so much about our lives. We have gone from a world of limited knowledge that was difficult for most to access to what is perceived by many as a world of unlimited knowledge and universally easy access.

Living in interesting times means that we live at a time when there are some very challenging problems to deal with too, and it is my experience with some of those challenges that has motivated this project in the first place. But I am getting ahead of myself, so please allow me to make a few points that are the foundation for what follows.

Point One

Though we will not concentrate on the challenges that have come along with our children's behavior over the last many years, it would seem important to give you some general background about what we have been up against. Not that we have experienced *everything* that could go wrong. We haven't. But we have had enough experience with bad decisions, over an extended period of time and involving all four of our children, to duplicate most of the issues that you might be facing in today's world. So I guess what I'm trying to say is, "Been there. Done that. Sold the T-shirt."

To put a bit finer point on that statement, here is a short list of things that we have not had to deal with: Satan worship, homosexuality, self mutilation, major eating disorders, actual suicide. I say actual suicide because we have heard talk of suicide on several occasions and from more than one child, and we are aware of one specific attempt at suicide.

Point Two

Next up is the fact that I believe our Church leaders, especially at the general level, fight a constant battle between saying too much and saying too little. In short, because their audience is so general it is almost impossible for them to be as direct as they might like.

As a "regular" Church member, I have no such limitation. Thus, it is my intent to speak as plainly as I am able, in the hope that doing so will help to open the eyes of your understanding and make you equal to the challenges that bring you to these pages in the first place. At the same time, many years of teaching Sunday School and other Church classes has taught me that humor can play a very important role in explaining different gospel concepts. So there will be places where I will try to use some humor to lighten the mood a little and to make different points in ways that I think can be helpful. In the immortal words of Mr. Spock of Star Trek fame, "Humor . . . a difficult concept."

Point Three

Though used infrequently, the specific family experiences referred to are very personal, so I have done everything I can to make it impossible to determine which of my children might have been involved in any of them. Thus, their actual names do not appear anywhere, and the names used are also gender neutral to make the personal pronouns a matter of grammatical correctness only. I trust that you will understand the need to respect the privacy of my family, for our children are adults now, and maintaining their privacy is the least I can do. They have also been asked to review and approve what follows, which means that they have had veto rights on everything contained here. There are a few minor changes that have been requested, and those requests have been honored to the letter. The same also holds true where examples are used from the lives of friends, or for the art therapy pictures that are part of Principle Four.

Point Four

I have long believed that if we properly understood all the ramifications of the scripture that says, "The power is in them wherein they are agents unto themselves," we could avoid or eliminate a large percentage of the frustration and unhappiness that plague the world today. What I mean is that if we *really* understood how much control we have over our personal, private, daily lives—what we think, how we feel, and how we react to our daily experiences—we would be absolutely stunned to discover how much power we have to make the changes that we think are needed in our lives.

So everything that follows is based on the general premise that it does not matter what the specific issue is, whether it be addiction in any of its forms or abuse in any of its forms or sexual problems in all of their forms or any others that you might care to list; all of these come about as a result of the thought processes that we allow to go on within our own mind, heart, and soul. This statement will be supported both doctrinally and psychologically, which just means that the issues addressed throughout this book are very controversial to some and very uncomfortable for others.

Point Five

While this work will rely heavily on the doctrines and scriptures of The Church of Jesus Christ of Latter-day Saints, it may be that someone not of our faith will find their way to its pages. If that is your case, please know that I will use what I believe are the best scriptural quotes that I can, regardless of their ancient or modern origin. It must also be stated that this book is *not* intended as a proselyting tool. It is merely an attempt to use my individual experience, the doctrines of our Church, and sound psychological principles to provide increased understanding, and thus reduce the almost unbearable pain and guilt that come from the kind of experiences that will be addressed throughout.

Point Six

Everything that follows is also based on the premise that it is possible to use both the doctrines of the restored gospel and sound psychological principles—what I like to refer to as practical thinking—to address the issues of the day. This approach is based on two different statements from Church leaders. The first comes from Elder Boyd K. Packer, who said, "True doctrine, understood, changes attitudes and behaviors . . . quicker than a study of behavior will improve behavior."[1] I support that statement and believe it to my very core, for it is my experience that this simple statement—if properly understood and applied—can do more to improve our lives than almost anything outside of John 17:3: "And this is life eternal, that they might know thee the only true God, and Jesus Christ, whom thou hast sent."

But there are two things that must be present for the changes indicated by this statement to be possible. First, the doctrine involved must be true, for nothing less than the purest form of truth can have the impact required to bring about the almost instantaneous changes that come when the Holy Ghost bears his powerful witness of any particular principle or truth. Second, the hearer must understand the true doctrine *before* the changes in attitudes and behavior can occur. This may seem like an obvious and unnecessary statement, but as you will find later on, it is virtually impossible to overstate the importance of what we understand versus the point at which we gain that understanding.

The latter part of the thirteenth article of faith simply says, "If there is *anything* virtuous, lovely, of good report, or praiseworthy, we seek after these things" (italics added). This statement is included to remind us that it is possible for truth to come from many different sources, and that though the prophets and apostles, both ancient and modern, are the best source of spiritual truth, they are not the only source.

There are those on all sides of the issues addressed throughout this book who typically turn to either one type of source or one specific source to the exclusion of all others. I find such an approach to be both shortsighted and terribly inefficient, and we must also never forget that truth is truth, regardless of its source. So please, let's not throw the baby out with the bathwater just because we don't like where something comes from.

So with that foundation in place, let's see if we can build something on it.

Where it all starts

One of the most moving and important spiritual experiences of my life occurred in the backseat of a Ford Pinto while driving down the street in Scottsdale, Arizona, my first area of labor as a full-time missionary. Over thirty years have passed since that day, but my best recollection is that this occurred in early 1976. I will never forget the feelings that came when I read D&C 58:26–33 for the first time. I know it was the first time I had ever read those verses because I had never read the Doctrine and Covenants before leaving on my mission, at least not with the intent of gaining understanding or personal guidance. These words may have reached my ears during a seminary or Sunday School class somewhere along the way, but this was the first time I was ever paying attention.

They read as follows:

> For behold, it is not meet that I should command in all things; for he that is compelled in all things, the same is a slothful and not a wise servant; wherefore he receiveth no reward.
>
> Verily I say, men should be anxiously engaged in a good cause, and do many things of their own free will, and bring to pass much righteousness;
>
> For *the power is in them*, wherein they are *agents unto themselves*. And inasmuch as men do good they shall in nowise lose their reward.
>
> But he that doeth not anything until he is commanded, and receiveth a commandment with doubtful heart, and keepeth it with slothfulness, the same is damned.
>
> Who am I that made man, saith the Lord, that will hold him guiltless that obeys not my commandments?
>
> Who am I, saith the Lord, that have promised and have not fulfilled?
>
> I command and men obey not; I revoke and they receive not the blessing.
>
> Then they say in their hearts: This is not the work of the Lord, for his promises are not fulfilled. But wo unto such, for their reward lurketh beneath, and not from above. (Italics added)

If I were to write a personal mission statement or philosophy of life, it would be based on these verses because since that day long ago in Scottsdale, I have known without any question that I alone am accountable for my thoughts, feelings, choices, and actions. In addition, the importance of not waiting for someone else to tell me what to do, but being anxiously engaged of my own free will, made a very strong impression on my mind and heart. I will never claim to have done an even semi-acceptable job of following through on those realizations, but that does not change my awareness of my own accountability.

Easy to say, you think. But is it hard to prove? Not if you are willing to accept the scriptures for what they say.

Notes

1. Boyd K. Packer, "Little Children," *Ensign*, Nov. 1986, 17.

1.2 Agency and the Plan of Salvation

IF WE ARE TO HAVE ANY CHANCE OF UNDERSTANDING God's plan for our earthly existence, we must go back to a point before the creation of this world. First we must expand our understanding of the conditions that we lived under while there, and then we must apply that understanding to our current condition.

One of the most important concepts that we will ever learn is that God, our Heavenly Father, is organized and orderly in everything that he does. In 1 Corinthians 14:33 we learn, "For God is not the author of confusion, but of peace." We also know that "all kingdoms have a law given; and . . . there is no space in the which there is no kingdom; and there is no kingdom in which there is no space, either a greater or a lesser kingdom. And unto every kingdom is given a law; and *unto every law there are certain bounds also and conditions.* All beings who abide not in those conditions are not justified" (D&C 88:36–39; italics added), meaning they cannot return to live in the presence of the Father. And finally, "There is a law, irrevocably decreed in heaven before the foundations of this world, upon which all blessings are predicated—And when we obtain any blessing from God, it is by obedience to that law upon which it is predicated" (D&C 130:20–21).

Virtually every parent in the world can identify with the feelings of frustration that come from being lied to by their child, and there are few things I have found to be more aggravating! Yet children, especially teenagers, are constantly trying to figure out where they fit in the world. As they go through that process, it is completely normal for them to challenge most of the things they have been taught since they were babies, but in most cases those challenges are not made directly because they fear the reaction that they would get from taking such a course. So instead, many do as they want and tell half-truths or outright lies to try to avoid the consequences that they know will follow.

Imagine the confusion that would rule the universe if our Heavenly Father were as fickle and unreliable as a teenager. At the very core of our ability to have faith in him is the absolute perfection with which he keeps his own laws. Which then means that he must also already know all things, because if there is anything he did not already know, if there is any new truth that he can come to understand, then the possibility exists for him to learn something that would be contrary to one of the laws he has already enacted and commanded us to keep. If that were to happen then what we understand to be one of the conditions of our salvation must irrevocably be changed, and God is no longer a being in whom we can have absolute faith.

So, at the top of our list of things we must understand if we are to have a chance of moving forward with any faith at all is the concept that God is reliable and unchangeable, and that as a result *we can predict with great accuracy what his response will be to any given situation*. We also must focus our attention on the fact that his responses—in the form of blessings—are guaranteed. If they were not, he would cease to be God. That is one of the meanings of the phrase "and unto every law there are certain bounds also and conditions."

But what do God's perfection, his knowledge of all things, and the keeping of his own laws have to do with agency, you ask?

Good question, so keep reading.

The second concept that we must understand if we are to know the character of God is the fact that there are a certain few eternal laws that exist simply because that is the way things are. Even God, the greatest of all, is subject to them simply because of his own existence, and if he were to try to change them, or if he disobeyed any of them, he would cease to be God.

Preeminent among these eternal laws is the absolute right of self-determination, or what is more commonly referred to as agency.

Agency, in its most simplified form, means that everything that ever has or ever will exist in all of eternity has the inherent right to decide for itself whether or not it will keep the laws that are required for that form of creation to fulfill its design and live forever in the presence of God, our Heavenly Father.

More plainly stated, agency has always existed, even before God was God, and the Father's willingness to abide by that law is one of the greatest hallmarks of his perfection.

Agency is *not* free, and may we please never hear the term *free agency* used again in the Church. In his masterful general conference address from April 1992, Elder Boyd K. Packer said it this way: "The phrase 'free agency' does not appear in scripture. The only agency spoken of there is moral agency."[1] What Elder Packer is trying to teach us is that every choice we ever make, regardless or how large or small, regardless of how consciously or unconsciously we make that choice, has consequences attached to it. In cases where we choose to conform to eternal laws, the consequences are good. When we choose to act in ways that are contrary to eternal law, the consequences are less positive. It can also be said that our good choices bring us closer to God and our evil choices take us away from him. And it is this process, getting closer to or further away from God, that makes it possible for the blessings and punishments to teach us, by our own undeniable experience, the difference between those things of eternal worth and those of lesser value.

In addition, as taught by King Benjamin, God "doth require that ye should do as he hath commanded you; for which if ye do, he doth immediately bless you" (Mosiah 2:24). And because everything has its opposite, it can then be said that when we break an eternal law the condemnation or punishment associated with that law is also immediate. The trick for us, in fact the whole purpose in our being here, is to learn to recognize the immediate blessing or punishment that we receive, and then correct our behavior so as to move back in a more positive direction.

I realize that it may seem ridiculous to talk of immediate blessing or immediate punishment. After all, there are too many examples of a lack of immediacy in our blessings or punishments to even consider such a concept. But it is my experience that Father means exactly what King Benjamin says in that scripture, and that there truly is an immediate reward or punishment for all of our thoughts, feelings, choices, and actions. That those rewards or punishments virtually always come in a spiritual form that cannot be defined by our physical senses does not make them any less real; it only means that we are less aware of them, and hence we do not recognize or understand the immediacy of most of our blessings or punishments.

So, agency has always existed, the right of self-determination is at the very heart of our gospel journey, and it has been so since before the world was created.

Agency means personal accountability.

Next on the list of doctrines that we must understand is the codependent nature of agency and personal accountability. It cannot be overstated how intertwined these doctrines are, and I am convinced that this relationship is at the very center of our existence, in either spirit or mortal form.

Without agency, without the absolute right of self-determination, there can be no personal accountability. Without agency, unless we actually have control over every individual decision that makes up our life's actions, it is impossible for us to be held accountable for those actions. Without the right to choose for ourselves, we could always fall back on the defense that someone else told us what to do, chose our course of action for us, or forced us to do something, anything, different from what we thought was best.

In view of the fact that agency has always existed, and that it is agency that makes it possible for us to be held accountable for *every* choice we make, is it not also obvious that the same accountability has been in place for far longer than our brief mortal probation here on this earth?

Why is it that what seem to be such basic doctrines must be explained in such minute detail, with such specificity? Because I believe that we are so bombarded with the relativistic thinking of the day that it muddles our thinking—even on something so basic as the doctrines of agency and personal accountability—to the point that there are many in the Church, let alone the rest of the world, who have been deceived into believing that they really do not have a choice in regard to some part of their life or another.

May I state categorically that this is the single greatest lie ever told by the greatest liar in all of eternity! Because if Satan can convince us that something is truly beyond our control, meaning that we really do not have a choice in the matter, he wins by default and there is, by extension, nothing we can do to combat any urge, temptation, or evil influence in our lives.

Simply stated, that is false doctrine of the highest order.

In today's modern world it seems that not a week can pass without some new scientific study being published to "prove" that every imaginable human behavior is based on genetics, environmental conditions, the way the stars lined up on the day we were born, the amount of money our parents either had or didn't have, how many siblings we had and where we fell in the birth order, or any one of at least a thousand other variables. Most would rather rely on these excuses than face the eternal truth that we alone are accountable for every action that we take or choice that we make. Not that circumstances and environments do not play an enormous role in our lives; it is obvious that they do. But even from a cursory review of scripture it should be just as obvious that "men will be punished for their own sins, and not for Adam's transgression" (second article of faith).

It is one of the great examples of the craftiness of the adversary that such an obvious statement raises the ire of so many in the world. Again quoting Elder Packer: "Interesting how one virtue, when given exaggerated or fanatical emphasis, can be used to batter down another, with freedom, a virtue, invoked to protect *vice.* Those determined to transgress see any regulation of their life-style as interfering with their agency and seek to have their actions condoned by making them legal."[2]

Notes

1. Boyd K. Packer, "Our Moral Environment," *Ensign*, Apr. 1992, 66.
2. Ibid.

1.3 Agency in the Premortal Existence

The Beginning of Opposition

IN OUR PREMORTAL SPIRIT FORM WE HAD THE opportunity to walk and talk with Father in Heaven, and it was plainly obvious to us that there were things he could do because of his body of flesh and bones that we could not do as spirits. We desired the ability to do those same things. I am sure that most of us, if not all of us, pestered him relentlessly for information and insight into what it was like for him to live his kind of life versus what we were then able to experience and understand.

Someone who hasn't experienced the never-ending question of "Why? Why? Why? Why?" coming from a young child can never appreciate what that must have been like for Heavenly Father. And it shouldn't be too tough to imagine his response after trying to explain those things the first few billion times. "Okay, I'm getting really tired of repeating this, so let's get everyone together in a big meeting where I can explain it one more time, and then we can get on with things."

Can you imagine the frustration of trying to explain physical experiences, emotions, and feelings to pure spirits? A few of the best comparisons I can think of are trying to explain in words the difference between salt and sugar, bitter and sweet, pleasure and pain, or light and darkness. The words are easy to say, but no matter how many you use, or how well chosen and descriptive the adjectives are, no amount of words or willingness to take the time to explain things can ever make the point as well as one taste of salt followed by another of sugar.

So, because of his perfection and his desire for us to be like he is, Father proposed that if we would keep the same laws that he does in the same ways that he does, we could become exactly as he is. He also explained that for us to do so, a world would have to be created where we could come to obtain a mortal body and have all of the experiences that we were asking for. Then he told us that it was critical for us leave him alone and stop pestering him for details that were impossible for him to explain to us in words. He also explained that because the learning experience needed to be as individual as possible, he would not be coming to earth with us, and that a veil of forgetfulness would be drawn over our minds while we were here so that we would not be able to use our experiences there to directly help us while we were away. In other words, we were going to have to learn by doing and experiencing things for ourselves without him looking over our shoulder all the time.

Do you think you were one of those who jumped to your spirit feet and shouted, "Sign me up! I'm game for whatever I have to go through to go there and get me some experience for myself." Or were you one of those looking around and asking, "Away? What's away, and why would I ever want to be someplace that you weren't, Father?"

What we are talking about here is another of those eternal laws that God did not put into place. We are describing the fact that all organized beings, especially those with higher reasoning capabilities, can get confused by things they do not understand, and that this confusion makes them unsure about what is the best way to proceed.

In other words, we are talking about opposition.

For the purposes of this discussion we will define opposition as any situation or set of circumstances that provides us with a choice between at least two different alternatives.

As that and subsequent meetings took place, Father's plan was explained in its entirety and we finally got to a point where nothing else could be gained by further talk or discussion. We had as much as we could get without actually implementing the plan and moving things forward.

But, in one of the most instructive experiences in all of eternity, Father still had the omnipresent law of agency that he had to live by if he was going to remain perfect. So he opened the meeting to something more than just teaching and explanation—he opened the meeting to debate. Here, for the first time, was the opportunity for each of us to make a definitive statement as to how we felt about the plan he was proposing.

Were you willing to accept his plan and subject yourself to separation from him in both physical and spiritual ways that were beyond your ability to understand? Had you developed enough understanding to realize that walking by faith would be as difficult as it has turned out to be? Were you among those who continued to ponder and fret about your ability to meet the standard that had been proposed?

With that as a backdrop, is it not then obvious that at least one of us would rise and offer complete support for the plan and be willing to do whatever it took to implement it in its entirety? And is it not just as obvious that at least one would rise in total opposition? The nature of some spirits is to be contrary and argumentative simply because they can, simply because they exist and think independently, and they do so without regard for the consequences of the thoughts and the actions that unavoidably follow them. So, our Heavenly Father did not create Satan and evil as some claim we teach; he simply continued to live by all of the eternal laws that make him God—agency and accountability foremost among them—and allowed Satan and his followers to simply suffer the consequences of their own actions.

Is it not horrifyingly obvious that Lucifer is the way he is by his own choice? Is it not blindingly obvious that, as a perfect being, God will force no spirit to do things his way, because to do so would make him less than perfect and would thereby make him a being in whom we could have no faith?

To me, there are no more chilling words in all of eternity than those spoken by Lucifer when he said, "Behold, here am I, send me, *I* will be thy son, and *I* will redeem all mankind, that one soul shall not be lost, and surely *I* will do it; wherefore give *me* thine honor" (Moses 4:1; italics added). Please take special note of the adversary's emphasis on his own efforts and the reward that he demanded as compensation. I have not the barest comprehension of the arrogance that it would take for a spirit, any spirit, to stand before a glorified and perfected being of flesh and bone, one who knows all things and has all power and authority, and demand that he give his glory and perfection to me because of anything that I had done.

But, sadly, such is the character—chosen by him and him alone—of the adversary.

And there is yet one other critical piece of light and knowledge that can come to us from the example of the adversary. God himself, through the instrumentality of his Beloved Son, has said, "Wherefore, because that Satan rebelled against me, *and sought to destroy the agency of man*, which I, the Lord God, had given him, and also that I should give unto him mine own power; by the power of mine Only Begotten, I caused that he should be cast down; And he became Satan, yea, even the devil, the father of all lies, to deceive and to blind men, and to lead them captive at his will" (Moses 4:3–4; italics added).

So, Lucifer sought to destroy the agency of man and in so doing tried to break the most basic law of heaven, and thus he fell, to become the devil and the father of all lies.

The next step in the plan—mortal creation

Once the question of whether we would support Jehovah or Lucifer had been answered, it was time to implement the program and move forward with the plan that Father had outlined. Of course that meant that some would move on to the next stage in the plan and that others would not. Those who chose to follow Lucifer have the only reward that their own choice could provide them, and those who chose to follow Jehovah were able to move forward with their opportunity to progress. Again, this ability to progress came about because of our individual choice, and for no other reason.

Next up in order of the things required to implement the plan was the creation of a mortal earth, someplace different and less exalted than where Father lived, so that we could receive our bodies and begin the process of gaining additional experience for ourselves.

Once again, order ruled the day and all things were done in a way that would allow each of us the best opportunity, given the individual preparation and inclinations that we had developed to that point, to gain the specific experiences that were needed to give each of us the best chance of returning and living in Father's presence again. Father took everything into account, especially the loyalty and devotion that we had already shown during the great debate already described, and chose those who would be his helpers in implementing the specifics of the plan.

Chief among those servants was the eldest of Father's spirit children, even the great Jehovah, he who had risen and offered himself as the sacrifice we had been told was at the very center of the plan. Standing at his side was Michael, the leader of those who had chosen to support Father's plan, and the one who had actually cast Lucifer out of Father's presence. It is also obvious that there were many others present, including the noble and great ones shown to Abraham (see Abraham 3:22–23). At this point it is sufficient to say that each of us was involved in this process to the degree that our faithfulness warranted. And once again, the laws of agency, accountability, and positive or negative reward were in full operation, and we were provided with as much information as we had proven ourselves capable of handling.

From that point Father, along with at least Jehovah and Michael, went through the processes of spiritual and physical creation. As a result, worlds were provided where each spirit who had chosen to support Father's plan could receive a physical body and experience mortality as a result of the choices they had already made.

1.4 Adam, Eve, and Opposition

Their Right to Choose

SINCE THE ENTIRE PLAN OF SALVATION RESTS ON THE three pillars of the Creation, the Fall, and the Atonement, it should be obvious that we need to understand as many of the experiences of Adam and Eve in the Garden of Eden as we possibly can. Yet it is my experience that there are few things outside the actual Atonement of Christ that are less understood than the Fall of Adam and Eve.

As a brief backup for that statement, consider the number of times you have sat in some church class or another and heard the subject of "contradictory commandments" brought up, and then recall the mass of confusion that follows.

If it were not so critical a subject, it would be great comedy.

But because it is so critical, because the experiences of Adam and Eve in getting to and through the Fall are so all encompassing and instructive, I believe that there is no gospel subject, other than the Atonement of Christ, that is more important for us to gain a complete understanding of.

Why is this so critical, you ask? Because it is my conviction that if we properly understand Adam and Eve's experiences in the garden, we will then have a proper context with which to frame our own process of gaining experience and dealing with the consequences of our choices—again, personal accountability—and not before.

As previously discussed, the conditions that prevailed in the Garden of Eden *had* to be set up the way that they were, or God himself would not have been able to keep the laws that were already in place, and he would thus cease to be God. Once again, this is the most instructive and important example of this concept that we have, because Adam and Eve's experiences in the garden are the single greatest mortal demonstration of Father's commitment to the eternal law of agency.

Rather than Adam and Eve having mortality thrust upon them as the result of some premortal choice that would not be remembered once the veil was drawn—there could be no learning from such a course—God simply gave them commandments that were in perfect harmony with the law of opposition in all things. Meaning that Adam and Eve were simply put in the position of being able to make the first choice, that choice being whether or not to partake of the fruit of the tree of knowledge of good and evil.

Why was it done this way, you ask? Because it was the only way that Father could allow them their own agency. Because it was the only way to have mortality brought upon them by their own actions, and thereby make it possible to hold them accountable for those actions. Simply stated, if mortality had come upon Adam and Eve in any other way, they would have rightly been able to claim force, coercion, or some other reason for a legitimate and honorable lack of accountability.

For the clearest explanation in all of the scriptures on this subject we turn to the words of Lehi, who said,

> And to bring about his eternal purposes in the end of man, after he had created our first parents, and the beasts of the field and the fowls of the air, and in fine, all things which are created, *it must needs be that there was an opposition*; even the forbidden fruit in opposition to the tree of life; the one being sweet and the other bitter. Wherefore, *the Lord God gave unto man that he should act for himself.* Wherefore, man could not act for himself save it should be that he was enticed by the one or the other. (2 Nephi 2:15–16; italics added)

In addition, please pay special attention to Adam and Eve's response when the Lord came to talk to them and they hid themselves because they had discovered their nakedness. Have you ever noticed that they made no attempt to deny what they had done? Having never experienced a consequence prior to that time, and because they were in a state of total innocence and were incapable of deceit or evasion, they simply admitted their actions and stood ready to accept whatever the result of their choice would be.

Imagine the shock to their minds and souls when they were told that they would be sent out of the garden. Imagine the even greater shock when they learned that they were now going to have to work for everything needed to sustain their new mortal bodies. Physical hunger is one of the most powerful experiences any of us will ever have, so imagine the first time hunger pangs came upon them and they realized the necessity of finding food, not for simple enjoyment as it had been before, but for life-sustaining nourishment.

Then imagine the greatest shock of all, that of being cast out of Father's presence and not being able to walk and talk with him as they had previous to their transgression. Having stood in his glorious presence for any time at all, how did they feel when that opportunity was now gone and they discovered that they were going to have to work just as hard for spiritual nourishment as they were for physical? (It must be noted that they retained full knowledge of their interaction with Father that took place before they partook of the fruit. For in their case—just as with us—the veil of forgetfulness was drawn when their spirits left Father's presence and entered their bodies, not when they left the garden.)

Then, with those thoughts in mind and remembering that this was only *after* their keeping of the commandment to build an altar and offer prayer, listen to how they respond to their first experience with the Holy Ghost.

First the Lord said,

> I am the Only Begotten of the Father from the beginning, henceforth and forever, that as thou hast fallen thou mayest be redeemed, and all mankind, even as many as will.
>
> And in that day Adam blessed God and was filled, and began to prophesy concerning all the families of the earth, saying: Blessed be the name of God, for because of my transgression my eyes are opened, and in this life I shall have joy, and again in the flesh I shall see God.
>
> And Eve, his wife, heard all these things and was glad, saying: Were it not for our transgression we never should have had seed, and never should have known good and evil, and the joy of our redemption, and the eternal life which God giveth unto all the obedient. (Moses 5:9–11; italics added)

No matter how difficult the trials have been, no matter how worried and frightened I have been as we have waited multiple days and nights for wayward children to finally contact us and let us know that they were still alive, no matter how awful the realizations of my own shortcomings as a parent have been, for some reason these words, and others that we will discuss later on, have been like a light set on a hill for me. As a result, I can say with total sincerity that even in the darkest of times I have been able to find comfort and relief in the refuge of the scriptures. I have usually been able to find some kind of silver lining among the storm clouds, and I learned long ago that asking myself a very simple question was usually the best way to distract my mind from the immediate problem.

That question is simply, What am I supposed to be learning from this specific experience?

In stumbling upon this approach, I like to think that I discovered one of the great secrets of life. At least it has become so for me. I do not say that because I believe I am special in any way; I say it because I have come to understand, at least in some small way, the feelings that Adam and Eve expressed as quoted above. I have come to the realization that no matter how painful the experience may be, and no matter how many times we have had virtually identical experiences with multiple children, there is always something new that I can learn, some new insight that Father is waiting to give me.

Through it all I have also come to understand that the major reason for repeated experiences, at least as they relate to my own life and choices, was my inability to figure out what it was Father was trying to teach me the first eight times, when I did something poorly. Then I am humbled as I realize yet again how well Father knows me and each of my children, and I am astonished at his ability to give each of us the experiences that are needed to make the most progress that we are capable of during our sojourn here in mortality.

For a slightly different approach to the experiences in the Garden of Eden and the negative connotation that is given to Eve by some who misunderstand Father's plan, consider the following perspective taken from an interesting book, *Finding Faith in the Desert*, by Anthony W. Horton. Brother Horton is an LDS chaplain serving in the Unites States Army, and the book deals with his experiences ministering to American solders while fighting in Iraq.

Brother Horton's suggestion is that when Adam answered the Lord's question about whether or not he had partaken of the fruit of the tree of knowledge of good and evil the way he did, he was in actuality giving Eve great credit for her involvement in the process. He says it this way,

> I suggested that Adam was honoring his good wife, Eve, and giving her the credit for enlightening him of the need to partake of the fruit, and then

> he, Adam, alone made the decision to eat, taking full responsibility for the decision.
>
> Somehow giving Eve credit took away the negative feelings those (officer) candidates had. One approached me later and humbly asked if I would tell him the story again so he could tell his wife, as he had never heard the story told quite like that before. It felt right, and somehow he felt good inside listening to and thinking about the events of the Garden of Eden. He told me that he never felt that Eve was to blame for our being here. He told me how he loved and cherished his mother and his wife and could not picture Eve in any less of a light. More importantly, he mentioned that it changed how he viewed life and the reason we are here on earth. *Somehow taking the blame away from Eve gave new meaning and purpose for his existence.*[1]

I believe that the reaction of that officer candidate validates the amount of space given to these concepts, because, as previously stated, I believe that when the light of true understanding dawns on our minds and hearts we are finally in a position where Father can teach us something to improve our lives.

And finally, please consider an anecdotal account of unknown origin that has found its way around the email universe of late. It puts forth a possible scenario as to the events in the garden.

> After creating heaven and earth, God created Adam and Eve. And the first thing he said was "DON'T!"
>
> "Don't what?" Adam replied.
>
> "Don't eat the forbidden fruit." God said.
>
> "Forbidden fruit? We have forbidden fruit? Hey, Eve . . . we have forbidden fruit!"
>
> "No way!"
>
> "Yes way!"
>
> "Do NOT eat the fruit!" said God.
>
> "Why?"
>
> "Because I am your Father and I said so!" God replied, wondering why he hadn't stopped creation after making the elephants.
>
> A few minutes later God saw his children having an apple break, and he was angry!
>
> "Didn't I tell you not to eat the fruit?" God asked.
>
> "Uh huh," Adam replied.
>
> "Then why did you?" said the Father.
>
> "I don't know," said Eve.

> "She started it!" Adam said
> "Did not!"
> "Did too!"
> "Did not!"
> Having had it with the two of them, God's punishment was that Adam and Eve should have children of their own. Thus the pattern was set and it has never changed.

And in what I think is one of the more insightful and important questions that will ever be put to us, the piece concludes with this little gem: "But there is reassurance in the story! If you have persistently and lovingly tried to give your children wisdom and they haven't taken it, don't be hard on yourself. If God had trouble raising children, what makes you think it would be a piece of cake for you?"

I love this anecdote for two reasons:

First, it gives wonderful insight into the "humanity" of God, our Father. It is written in a way that is easy for me to relate to, for it is written from the same perspective that I have with my own children, and that makes it easier for me to put Father's feelings into a context that I can also relate to. It also makes it easier for me to try to adapt my own parenting approaches to more closely mirror Father's, so that I can try to use the same techniques that he does to gain the same results.

Second, it points out the critical fact that God, the greatest of all, has less than perfect children *and is still able to remain God.* So what makes me think that I could ever be a better parent than he is?

Is this not the greatest demonstration in all of eternity that we will each be held responsible for our own actions and choices? This concept proves to us that while we are responsible to properly teach our children of God's existence and the basic laws that they are accountable for, they alone bear the responsibility for their actions and choices.

It should be obvious that we will spend a great deal more time addressing this question later on, but there are other things to be put in place first.

So, let us move on.

Notes

1. Anthony W. Horton, *Finding Faith in the Desert* (Provo, UT: Spring Creek Books, 2004), 63; italics added.

Principle Two

This Life Is a Test

2.1 Father's Plan for Our Salvation

WE BEGAN OUR JOURNEY TOGETHER BY REFERRING TO the statement, "May you live in interesting times." And so we do. But could there ever be a better description of the times we live in than this one: "Woe unto them that call evil good, and good evil; that put darkness for light, and light for darkness; that put bitter for sweet, and sweet for bitter! Woe unto them that are wise in their own eyes, and prudent in their own sight! Woe unto them that are mighty to drink wine, and men of strength to mingle strong drink: Which justify the wicked for reward, and take away the righteousness of the righteous from him!" (Isaiah 5:20–23).

When you read that, at least if you're paying any attention at all, there is a good chance you will conclude that Isaiah really was a prophet. Then read through this statement from a more modern source and see if it doesn't give you a little more clarity about the time we live in.

> We live in a day when the adversary stresses on every hand the philosophy of instant gratification. We seem to demand instant everything, including instant solutions to our problems. We are indoctrinated that somehow we should always be instantly emotionally comfortable. When that is not so, some become anxious—and all too frequently seek relief from counseling, from analysis, and even from medication. It was meant to be that that life would be a challenge. To suffer some anxiety, some depression, some disappointment, even some failure is normal. Teach our members that if they have a good, miserable day once in a while, or several in a row, to stand steady and face them. Things will straighten out. There is great purpose in our struggle in life.[1]

I'll grant you that when this statement was made almost thirty years ago we didn't know everything that we do now about depression or anxiety or ADD or any one of a laundry list of other legitimate ailments and mental health conditions. Nor is there quite the same stigma attached to seeking help from appropriate medications or qualified mental health practitioners that there used to be, nor should there be.

However, that does not change the validity of Elder Packer's statement in any fashion. It is just as accurate today as it was on the day it was said, probably even more so. But we don't like the challenges that life throws at us. We hate the fact that we don't always know the "right" choice to make at the drop of a hat, and we really hate the consequences that are attached to our poor choices.

What, did you really think that life was going turn out to be the fairy tale of your youth? Do you still think that it's all about "happily ever after," or is it just that you don't recognize all of those challenges for the learning experiences that they really are?

And no, I'm not asking those questions just to remind you of how miserable your life is and get you all depressed. I'm asking them to get you thinking about why we are here in the first place.

Oops, sorry. I'm getting ahead of myself again. Before we start trying to answer some of the most difficult questions in all of mortality, it might help to go back over a few more of the basics first.

As the result of our individual choice to support Father's plan for our progression, we have been given the privilege of coming here to earth and receiving a mortal body, and, as we are now quite aware, mortality is an experience filled with daily choices, challenges, and a wide variety of learning experiences. For some of us, the challenges began almost immediately, and for others they don't become quite so obvious until at least a little more time has passed. But come they do, and they do so because they are the best way—ultimately the only way—for us to learn the specific lessons that we each need. For only by learning those lessons will we be given the best opportunity of returning to Father's presence prepared to live as he does for all of eternity.

I have long been fascinated by our reaction to the challenges that mortality brings. By now it should be apparent to all of us that no matter what the circumstance, there are as many responses as there are individuals, and with only a small amount of reflection we should realize that it could be no other way. For if God is going to allow each of us the right to choose everything for ourselves, it should then be just as obvious that each of us will have a very individual, and at least somewhat different, reaction to any given experience. As a result, there are some very interesting and pointed questions that arise from our shared experience called life.

Some of the most frequently asked questions in all of mortality are:

- Why is life so difficult?
- Is it ever going to get any easier?
- Did I really agree to this?
- How much did I know before about what my life would be like here?
- Did I choose who my parents and children were going to be?
- If I am trying to live righteously, why do I have so many problems?

It has already been established in this and many other places that our Father in Heaven is a being in whom we can have absolute faith. It is also my experience that there are several additional doctrinal concepts that, when attached to that most basic of all truths, have given me a perspective that I find very comforting.

Foremost among these additional doctrines is the fact that it is impossible for Father to lie to us.

It is imperative to keep this concept very near the top of my list of things that we must know about God because if it were possible for him to lie to us, then he would immediately cease to be perfect, which would then mean that he was a being in whom we could not have faith unto salvation. These words from Paul make the point very clear: "Wherein God, willing more abundantly to shew unto the heirs of promise the immutability of his counsel, confirmed it by an oath: That by two immutable things, in which it was *impossible* for God to lie, we might have a strong consolation, who have fled for refuge to lay hold upon the hope set before us" (Hebrews 6:17–18; italics added). And further, let's add these words from the brother of Jared: "For thou art a God of truth, and canst not lie" (Ether 3:12).

Remember who it is that is the father of all lies, and then remember who is trying to persuade you that a particular situation is beyond your control—beyond your ability to deal or cope with.

Please carefully consider the following scripture as you ponder on this concept. "There hath no temptation taken you but such as is common to man: but God is faithful, who will not suffer you to be tempted above that ye are able; but will with the temptation also make a way to escape, that ye may be able to bear it" (1 Corinthians 10:13).

There are several great truths taught in this short verse, but in my mind there are two key thoughts that Paul gives us here.

First, when Paul says that there is no temptation but those that are common to man, I believe that he is telling us in a very specific and personal way that we are not alone in our mortal experiences. Paul is simply telling us that because of a severely limited perspective, our experiences seem totally unique to us, but that in fact they are no more nor less than those visited upon a large enough number of our fellow men so as to be called common.

I can only speak for myself, but I find great comfort in the fact that in the quiet places of my soul I am very little different from you, or anyone else for that matter. Which goes back to what should be one of the foundational thinking principles of our lives, in that we are all more or less the same, in that we all have concerns and problems. Yes, there are many differences in each of our lives, but the day-to-day process of living life is only intended to give each of us the individualized experiences that will best prepare us to return to live in Father's presence again. So my trials are my own, and they are no harder for me to bear than yours are for you. A good friend of mine says it this way: "One person's hangnail is another person's severed limb."

Second, in one grand and glorious sentence fragment, Paul teaches us one of the most profound truths in all of eternity. Namely, that it is impossible for us to be tested, tried, or as he says it, tempted, beyond our ability to resist.

Why is that so important, you ask? Because if it were possible for us to be tempted or tried beyond our ability to resist, our agency would then have been taken from us and we truly would no longer be able to make a choice, for the choice would then have been made for us. As a result, we would be in the position of rightly claiming that it truly was beyond our ability to control our action, and that because we had no real choice in the matter we cannot then be held accountable for that choice or action.

Does this line of thinking sound at all familiar to you? Do you remember who it was that wanted to take our agency from us before the world was even created, so that we would have to do things his way? Do you recognize the insidious and evil nature of the idea that we do not have a choice in any specific area of our lives? There are obviously those who truly do not have a choice, those of diminished capacity, those who are without the ability to reason beyond the age of accountability and without the ability to recognize the consequences of their actions. But, unless you fall into that category, there will come a time when you will be held accountable for the choices, actions, and course of your life.

Yes, that is a bold statement, and one that causes great consternation and debate, even among those who claim to know the fullness of the truth. But that does not change the reality of God's plan.

Does anything happen by chance?

While it might seem absurdly basic to raise this question, over the years I have found a surprisingly large number of people who either do not understand the importance of its answer, or who overlook the comfort that can come by keeping that answer near the top of their "answers to basic gospel questions" list.

As previously discussed, God is a being of perfect order and the ultimate keeper of every eternal law. Which then means that his actions and reactions are very predictable. If we consider just a couple of other basic concepts, it should become clear that it is impossible for anything to happen to you by chance.

Again, why is that idea so important, you ask?

Because if it were possible for *anything* to happen without Father's foreknowledge, we would be put back in the position of having the possibility of something he didn't or couldn't know about changing one of the established conditions of our obtaining salvation, and he would then be a being in whom we could not have faith sufficient unto salvation.

So the Father of us all has specific knowledge of everything that has ever happened to you in your life or that ever will happen to you. Then, because I know without question that God knows and loves me as an individual—in exactly the same way he knows and loves his Only Begotten Son and all of the holy prophets of all eternity—I can have both faith and confidence in the fact that my life is in his hands and will follow the course that is best suited to my individual needs. And if that is the case for me, then because God is no respecter of persons it must also be the case for you too.

An example: A few years ago a young man—who had grown up in our ward, filled an honorable mission, and then married—had just begun a family. He was in his mid twenties, the eldest in the family, and had done everything "right" to that point in his life. He was as big, strong, and robust as any young man could ever hope be, and he had a wonderful testimony of Jesus Christ as our Savior and of the restored gospel.

After a few weeks of not feeling particularly well but not specifically sick, he collapsed and was taken to the hospital, where he lapsed into a coma. Doctors were unable to determine the cause of the problem, and his condition deteriorated over a period of about three weeks until he passed from mortality. After his passing, it was discovered that he had lymphoma, which had created a cancerous mass behind the abdominal wall, and that there was nothing that could have been done to save him, regardless of a correct diagnosis or any additional treatment that might have been given.

He left a young wife with a three-month-old child, as devastated a father and mother as I have ever seen, and all of the terrible questions associated with such a tragedy.

The pain they were suffering was obvious, to the point that his father asked me some rhetorical questions at the viewing: "Why not take me? I've lived most of my life, and he still had his in front of him. Why does it have to happen this way?"

I will never forget the testimony meeting shortly thereafter when I stood at the pulpit and read the following scripture:

> And whosoever among you are sick . . . the elders of the church, two or more, shall be called, and shall pray for and lay their hands upon them in my name; and if they die they shall die unto me, and if they live they shall live unto me . . . And it shall come to pass that those that die in me shall not taste of death, for it shall be sweet unto them; . . . And again, it shall come to pass that he that hath faith in me to be healed, *and is not appointed unto death*, shall be healed. He who hath faith to see shall see. He who hath faith to hear shall hear. (D&C 42:43–50; italics added)

There were a great many tears shed that day, but I will always treasure the memory of the young man's father coming to me after the meeting and asking for the reference quoted above. My intent was simply to teach a little truth and, by doing so, provide some comfort. Comfort not by making their son's passing any less painful—such a thing is not possible—but comfort in the fact that our Heavenly Father had intimate knowledge of the situation and was in complete control of the end result, comfort in the fact that things had happened the way they did for reasons that make complete sense in the grand scheme of things, and comfort in the fact that God was still in absolute control and that all was still somehow right in the universe.

His father and I have never talked privately of this experience, but there have been a few occasions when he has quoted this scripture or made reference to it in some fashion. He has then said something to the effect that it has given him perspective and comfort, and that even though he does not yet fully understand why things had to happen the way they did, it has made it possible for him to carry on in faith and with the confidence that all is as it should be.

Our challenges—no, not all of them, just a few to help make the point

After serving an honorable mission, I came home and began the process of living the rest of my life. After meeting a wonderful young woman and being sealed to her in the Manti Temple, we began our lives together with all of the expectations that a young couple in that situation could have. We have been blessed with four children and have had most of the expected experiences that go with raising four intelligent and active children.

Virtually every family has at least one child who could be described as at least difficult, the one who is harder to deal with than all the others, and there are many who have dealt with a seriously wayward child, one who makes dangerous decisions that bring great fear and grief to their parents. In every home there are the normal issues and challenges that each and every child faces, because those experiences are the best way for Heavenly Father to teach us the things we need to know before we can return to his presence. But in our home it has not been one, two, or even three, but all four who have made decisions that have caused terrible fear, many sleepless nights, floods of tears, mountains of frustration and anger, and the kind of self-doubt and recrimination that only those who deal with serious and potentially life threatening choices must endure.

At the forefront of our challenges is the scourge of illegal drugs and the devastation that they bring to the lives of young and old throughout modern society.

As our kids grew and developed, it seemed to me that we had a reasonably happy home, one where my wife and I were truly devoted to each other and our children, and one where the gospel of Jesus Christ was at the center of our lives. Not that we have been perfect in our adherence to the counsel regarding weekly family home evenings or daily scripture study. We have not. However, we have done a reasonable job of having daily family prayers, blessings on the food at meals, weekly attendance at Church meetings, and most of the other recommended steps that are so conducive to helping children avoid the major obstacles to safe and healthy development. And because our kids have always been at the center of our lives, we have made significant sacrifices to ensure that their mother has been at home to provide the nurturing environment and security that are so essential to a child's development and happiness.

I have never expected that my children would naturally do things the way I did, nor have I expected that they would even want to. I have tried to encourage them to figure out what their own dreams were and then to follow them as positively and successfully as they could. We have not demanded straight As on report cards, perfect attendance at school or church, or participation in athletics, music, dance or any other extra curricular activity. In fact, because of limited funds our children have not been able to participate in those activities as much as they or I might have liked, which has created large questions in my own mind about how effective I have been as both a provider and teacher for my children. And much to my chagrin, there is one personality trait that came from my father that has been perpetuated, in that I have been far too authoritarian in my manner and bearing with my children. It has been far too easy for me to fall back on the same harsh tone of voice and demanding attitude that I was raised with in my interaction with my own children, and I fear that this is a major contributing factor to the problems and trials that we have been through.

As our kids reached their teens, we began to experience most of the different emotions and parent-child experiences that are a part of that most difficult time in our lives. I remember well some of the battles that I had with my own parents as I began to try to assert my own growing independence, and at least some of those same battles have occurred here in our home. Throughout that process I have always been aware of my own limitations and shortcomings, and I have constantly tried to give my kids the best counsel and advice that I could, while still recognizing that they truly are "agents unto themselves," and that I had very little control of what they would do or how well or poorly they would do it.

Our more serious problems began when one child started experimenting with marijuana in the mid-teen years and then began not only sharing information about this, but also began glamorizing it to the point of providing it and instruction to younger siblings.

The list of drugs involved is impressive by any standard; it includes virtually every drug that you may have heard of, and at least a couple that you probably haven't. We have also dealt with an unwed pregnancy and a couple of significant scares that others were imminent. Fortunately for all involved, the pregnancy has resulted in a delightful grandchild who brings joy and happiness to our entire family.

I mention those things at this point in our journey simply to establish some of the basic facts of what has happened here in our home, and to lay a little more groundwork for what will follow. But for now we need to continue with our examination of the nature of this test that we call mortality.

Notes

1. Boyd K. Packer, "Solving Emotional Problems in the Lord's Own Way," *Ensign*, May 1978, 93.

2.2 The Hard Questions

IN THE LAST CHAPTER THERE WAS A LIST OF frequently asked questions. With the examples of difficult experiences from my home and my dear neighbors in losing their son, we are now ready to address those questions more specifically.

So, why is life so difficult?

I think that the initial answer to this question is fairly simple and straightforward, in that life is so difficult simply because it has to be so. If we use the lives of a good majority of God's prophets and chosen leaders as examples, it should quickly become obvious how many of them have been tested and tried to the utmost farthing. From there it would seem to be a short step to again restate the fact that God is no respecter of persons, and that the end result of that fact is that none of us will get out of this life with any fewer or less intense trials than those chosen to lead us have had. Simply put, if God does not spare his chosen servants—or even his Only Begotten Son—from all of the travails, pain, and misery of mortality, what would ever make us think that we would have less of a test than they did?

And no, it isn't going to get easier. In fact, I would suggest that it will only get harder as we draw ever closer to the glorious return of our Savior, Jesus Christ.

Like I said, it's a fairly simple answer. But when we ask the same one-word question that our young children use to drive us nuts, things get significantly more complicated.

Yes, that question is, Why? Why does it have to be this way, and isn't there any other way for us to learn the lessons that Father is trying to teach us?

As you read that question, do you struggle to come up with an answer, or do you think back to some of what we reviewed in the chapters of Principle One? I am specifically referring to the concepts about trying to teach pure spirits about the nature of physical experience when there was no possible frame of reference. Oh sure, we had the best teacher in all of eternity, but it was still impossible for us to really get it until after we had become mortal and began to experience physical sensations and emotions for ourselves.

To frame this issue in a more understandable context, think of how many times you told your two- or three-year-old child to stay away from the hot stove before he actually got up on a counter, saw the pretty red burner, and reached out and touched it. Prior to that moment, all of your warnings had been a theoretical exercise, but once contact had been made, theory was out the window and your child—or maybe it was actually you—suddenly knew the reason for all the warnings. It is usually a matter of microseconds before the pain begins to register in our brain, and from that instant forward we can never again claim that we do not know what the result of touching a red-hot stove will be.

So it is with our lives. Once we have had a particular experience or trial, we can never again claim that it didn't happen, and if we are but willing to ask some questions and do a little searching for the answers, Father has promised that he will not leave us comfortless and without resources. In fact, he has promised that if we will "ask with a sincere heart, with real intent, having faith in Christ, he will manifest the truth of it unto you, by the power of the Holy Ghost. And by the power of the Holy Ghost ye may know the truth of *all* things" (Moroni 10:4–5; italics added). Notice that he does not say that you may know the truth of a few things or most things, but he says that you may know the truth of *all* things.

Now here is the really interesting question. Do you *really* believe that? Do you really believe that Father stands ready to answer *all* your questions? Do you really believe that God is no respecter of persons, or do you impose a limit on his power by making the decision that you are so insignificant or unworthy that your own eternal Father in Heaven is not interested enough in your life to reach out and give you the help that you so desperately need? I would suggest that this is precisely what a large percentage of us do when we get frustrated by the difficulty of the path that we are on. We figuratively throw our hands in the air by ceasing to read the scriptures and then pray for insight and understanding, and we thereby miss some of the greatest learning experiences that Father has laid before us.

Please never ever forget that we have been told, "Ye receive no witness until after the trial of your faith" (Ether 12:6). When you read that, I hope you come to the conclusion that at least Father understands the fact that it is only *after* a particular experience—think of touching the hot stove—that we really understand what he is trying to teach us.

A little further on in Ether chapter 12 we find these gems of insight and instruction: "And if men come unto me I will show unto them their weakness. I give unto men weakness that they may be humble; and my grace is sufficient for all men that humble themselves before me; *for if they humble themselves before me, and have faith in me, then will I make weak things become strong unto them*. Behold, I will show unto the Gentiles their weakness, and I will shown unto them that faith, hope and charity bringeth unto me—the fountain of all righteousness" (Ether 12:27–28; italic added).

So once again we are taught with exquisite clarity the fact that all of our lives—yes, even yours—are developing exactly as they must for us to learn the individual lessons that are the most important to each of us. Simply stated, each of us is having experiences that are tailored to our own individual needs and to our very individual learning styles, because that is the *only* way for us to learn the things we must.

So stop touching the red-hot burner already!

How much did we really know in advance?

Next up on our list of life's hard questions are three real doozies:

- Did I really agree to this?
- How much did I know before about what my life would be like here?
- If I am trying to live righteously, why do I have so many problems?

From the perspective we have now—think mortal, time centered, and without a clear memory of what went on before—it is very easy to say that if things had been explained to us in any detail at all we would never have agreed to what our lives have turned out to be. However, making that claim flies in the face of everything that we have already discussed. Hopefully you are beginning to recognize the fact that trying to make that claim is a very lazy and self-serving approach to life and the challenges that we encounter on a daily basis.

Why, you ask? Because it presupposes that we know more about what is best for us than Father does.

Even more important, I hope that thoughts of cause and effect, daily experience as a learning tool, the absolute rule of eternal laws, and Father's personal interest in your life are beginning to take hold in your heart and mind. But how are the questions at hand affected by those kinds of thoughts? I'm glad you asked.

It seems to me that if we have a correct understanding of the plan of salvation, of the purpose of this life and mortality, that the result of that understanding is a much more eternal perspective. And that eternal perspective then makes it easier for us to accept the challenges of mortality as opportunities for growth and progress, rather than either a daily drudgery or some kind of special daily hell that we just have to grit our teeth and endure.

As further clarification, here is a quote from Elder Neal A. Maxwell that seems appropriate. He said,

> Elder Orson Hyde said of our life in the premortal world, "We understood things better there than we do in this lower world." Elder Hyde also surmised as to the agreements we made there as follows: "It is not impossible that we signed the articles thereof with our own hands—which articles may be retained in the archives above, to be presented to us when we rise from the dead, and be judged out of our own mouths, according to that which is written in the books."
>
> Just because we have forgotten, Elder Hyde said, "our forgetfulness cannot alter the facts" (Brigham Young, *Journal of Discourses*, 7:314–315). . . . The degree of detail involved in the covenants and promises we participated in at that time may be a more highly customized thing than many of us surmise. Yet, on occasion, even with our forgetting, there are inklings. President Joseph F. Smith wrote: "But in coming here, we forget all, that our agency might be free indeed, to choose good over evil, that we might merit the reward of our own choice and conduct. But by the power of the Spirit, in the redemption of Christ through obedience, we often catch a spark from the awakened memories of the immortal soul, which lights up our whole being as with the glory of our former home" (Gospel Doctrine, pp. 13–14).[1]

As I have reflected on these questions, I have come to the conclusion that no matter how specific the details about some of our coming challenges were, *it did not reduce our enthusiasm for those details or challenges by even one iota*. There are two reasons for this.

First, we are back to the idea of trying to explain physical experiences to spirit beings, and by now it should be obvious that without a proper frame of reference that is something that is impossible for even God to do. But for a little more concrete approach, think of looking at pictures of the Colosseum in Rome versus actually standing in the arena.

Second, we were so excited at the opportunity to come here and gain a mortal body for ourselves (remember that this is the *only* way for us to gain the experience that we need if we are to become like Father) that we would have agreed to anything—literally—if he would just allow us to come here. Furthermore, I am convinced that the specifics of our circumstances here are based on the faithfulness we exhibited there, and that our preparation and demonstrated ability to deal with the challenges that were to be laid before us make it possible for us to deal with those challenges in a way that will be to the benefit and instruction of all involved.

All that is required is a willing spirit and a desire to learn from everything that happens in our lives.

A specific note of caution must be sounded here too. Please do not make the mistake of taking what you have just read to the extreme and false idea of predestination. By now it should also be obvious that "fate," something that was or is going to happen regardless of any initiative or choice on your part, is simply another way of saying that you have no agency and that you cannot be held accountable for your actions. Once again, that is false doctrine of the highest order, and that kind of thinking has no place in this discussion.

What we are talking about—yes, again—is the fact that Father knows us far better than we know ourselves. We are again talking about the fact that our lives—each of us as individuals—are following the path that will best prepare us to return and live again in his presence, and the more I reflect on that idea the more convinced I become of the very individual nature of the tests and trials that we are each asked to deal with. I find great peace of mind and spirit in the knowledge that my tests are mine, yours are yours, and neither of us will be asked to answer for the choices or lives of another. I also find great personal peace in the idea that I was not only given a significant amount of information about the course of my life in advance, but that I also made a conscious decision to accept the challenges that are now mine, and that that decision was possible because of the eternal law of agency *and because of my ability to recognize the blessing that it would be for me follow and accept Father's recommendations.*

So I guess the easiest way to express this is simply to say that I have no one but myself to blame for the difficulty of the path because I know that I not only agreed to it, but that I was ecstatic at the opportunity. Which then brings us to the last of the hard questions raised earlier.

Did we choose our parents and children?

Warning. Warning. Danger, Will Robinson. Danger. Personal opinion directly ahead!

Okay, if you're not old enough to remember the sixties TV show *Lost in Space*, you won't recognize that as being at least a little bit funny, but give an old guy a break for at least trying.

In all of my years of gospel study I am not aware of anything in the scriptures that addresses this question, nor am I aware of a definitive statement by any of the prophets or apostles of this dispensation, at least not any more definitive than those already quoted from Elders Hyde, Smith, and Maxwell. So, what follows is nothing more than personal opinion, and it should be taken as such. These thoughts are included here because I find comfort and focus by applying them to my individual life.

For me, because of the perfectly predictable pattern of Father's actions and reactions to any given set of circumstances, because of the preeminent importance of family in our mortal experience, given the eternal law of agency and its effects on everything that I have ever done or ever will do, and because we are talking about the eternal salvation of *my* soul here, I find it incomprehensible to think that I was not at least somewhat involved in the process of determining a large percentage of my experiences here in mortality. Included at the very top of the list of things I was made aware of and involved in the decision-making about was who my parents, wife, and children would be. I believe it is completely beyond reason to think that I could come from an existence based on agency, cause and effect, and increased blessings and responsibilities because of my choices, only to have some of the most critical events in my entire eternal journey determined by random chance.

So because I believe I was involved with Father in determining *some* of the conditions and specifics of my mortal test—and as with everything else we have or will discuss in this book—I am left without recourse when it comes to my ability to rightly complain about the unfairness or harshness of the test that I am now in the middle of. If things did in fact happen as they have been described above, then I must realize that I was not only involved in the process, but *I actually agreed to it and had to accept it in advance of my coming here.* And if that is the case, I must then come to the conclusion that after everything had been explained to me I made the conscious choice to agree to what was being proposed. In short, I am convinced that I am where I am, and involved with the people that I am, because I chose to accept the terms and conditions that came with the people involved. Which then means that I believe that I knew in advance a good percentage of the challenges that I would be facing. I further believe I was willing to accept them because of two very specific conditions.

First, I believe that I agreed to this path because I trusted Father enough to accept his version of the course that my life should take. I believe that there was a close enough relationship between the great God of the universe and me as an individual that we talked extensively about the different options that were available. I believe that the options that were available to me were based on my faithfulness to that point, and I believe that I chose to accept this path because I came to the conclusion that it was the best possible way for me to learn the things I needed to learn to allow me to return to Father prepared to live in his presence for the rest of eternity.

As an example of what this process might have entailed, just think of helping a child complete a class schedule for high school. This process typically includes sitting down with both the child and the catalogue of classes that are offered. Some classes are required for graduation, and some are electives that are intended to provide a child with a broader learning experience by exposing them to new ideas and new challenges. Sound familiar?

So I think it's fair to say that we probably had the same experience with Father, or at least something very similar to it.

Can you hear the conversation? "Alan, I think that because of your level of faithfulness here with me it would be a good thing for you to find out how serious you really are about following me through *anything* that might come your way. You have done an acceptable job of it while walking here by my side, but let's see how you do when you can't see me and can't use that sight to gain the confidence to continue on that path."

"But, Father, there isn't anything that could take me away from your side. I love you too much, and I will support your plan for my salvation to the ends of eternity."

"Yes, I know that's the reaction while we sit here together, but what will happen when I'm not there to personally support you? What will you do when things get tough, and I'm not there for you to see and watch?"

"Father, it will not matter how difficult the test is, I will *never* stray from the path that you have laid before me here."

And so we could go on for a very long time, but you get the point.

Second, I also believe that even if I did not specifically choose my parents, I at the very least agreed to go to the home that I did because of the specific lessons that would be learned in that home. I further believe that the same process repeated itself with my wife and children, and once again, we each made the agreements that we did because of the specific lessons that we would learn from being so closely associated with each other here in mortality.

So, we are where we are by, at a minimum, our own acceptance. The choices that were and are available to us were and are based on our faithfulness. We did have a far greater amount of involvement and input in the decision making process than we might have ever thought of before, *and we are left without the right to complain about the harshness or difficulty of the test because we agreed to it in advance.*

End of personal opinion section, and we now return you to your regularly scheduled programming.

Notes

1. Neal A. Maxwell, "Meeting the Challenges of Today" (devotional, Brigham Young University, Provo, UT, Oct. 10, 1978).

2.3 My Parable of the Bicycle

I HAVE BEEN AN AVID RECREATIONAL CYCLIST FOR OVER fifteen years now, and while they may not be immediately obvious, I have found that there are a great many direct parallels between riding a bike and living life. What follows is my attempt to explain those parallels in an understandable fashion.

When I talk of riding a bike I'm not talking about just rolling around the neighborhood or going to the corner grocery store for a gallon of milk, I'm talking about riding a racing bike over longer periods of time, at higher speeds, and over whatever naturally occurring obstacles might end up in the way on any given day. As long as there is pavement, you should be able to ride there. While I have never been a racing cyclist, I do enough riding each year to be able to hold a respectable pace on flatter terrain, and I can usually drag myself up most of the longer and steeper climbs that are available in the Wasatch Front area.

But how can riding a bicycle be a direct parallel to how you live your life? Once again, I'm glad you asked.

If you choose to do so, living life is something that can be done with a limited amount of contact with others. Most people would agree that life is not nearly as rewarding or enjoyable when tried that way, but it can be done nevertheless. Riding a bike is very much the same because it can be done alone or in groups, and most riders will tell you that riding with a group is not only more enjoyable, but more challenging too. There are several reasons this is the case:

- It is possible to go faster, and for a longer period of time, with a group than by myself.
- Attention is paid to everyone in the group, which helps us maintain a safe environment.
- The workload is shared by taking turns at the front of the paceline.
- Weaker riders are helped and protected throughout the ride.
- Newer riders gain skills and experience because they have stronger and more experienced riders there to push them beyond their current capabilities.
- And the most basic law in all of cycling—there is *always* somebody stronger than you are.

Also, please notice that I haven't even mentioned racing here. We are just talking about people like me, an old guy who loves competing with myself and spending time with friends who love riding as much as I do. I could spend lots of time expanding on just these basic items, but the parallels should be pretty obvious without extra commentary, and there are several other parallels that I think might be more to the point.

Riding a bike at a higher level than you might have tried before requires an interesting combination of physical strength, cardiovascular fitness, mental toughness, and a willingness to suffer, because, even at its most basic level, pain is a very real part of cycling. Swimming, cross-country skiing, and running are about the only sports that I know of with as much repetitive motion as cycling, but because the duration of those sports is so much shorter than a basic bike ride, they don't usually generate the amount of suffering that riding does. I'm not talking about overall fitness here—these athletes are some of the fittest people on the planet—but when you compare their longest duration events to a six- or seven-hour bike ride or race, you start to get the picture.

It is always interesting to see the reaction when I tell someone that I went for an eighty-mile ride that morning. First there is the shocked question: "How far?" Then it's common to get questions about how long it took—between four and a half and five hours, unless I'm with a group; how I am feeling—great, most of the time; how few brain cells I have left—not many; how does my rear end stand that much time in the saddle—years of conditioning, but very well actually; and you can probably guess the rest from there.

There was a time when I was just as incredulous as you are when I heard of such a ride, and there was also a time when the idea of trying to ride fifty miles caused me to break out in a cold sweat. But that was before I had ever tried any of those things.

Kind of like life, don't you think?

Now before heading out for a Saturday morning ride my questions have a lot more to do with how fast the pace will be and what mountains will be climbed than they do with distance. As long as I know at least some of the people involved—it is always critical to know when you are in over your head before something even starts—I can get a pretty good gauge on what kind of day it will be. And there are some groups I won't even attempt to ride with because I know I'm not strong enough to even hang on the back.

Another great truth of cycling is that the only thing worse than killing yourself to hang on to a fast group is letting them go and getting isolated by yourself. Riding by myself when doing regular training is one thing, but when riding with a group the speeds always go up, which means that the energy expended goes up too. But being by yourself when you are exhausted is no fun at all, and it makes for a very long and painful ride back to the car too.

Once again, just like life.

I have been riding long enough now to know that a huge percentage of the general population under fifty years of age could ride for at least fifty miles, and most of them could go for seventy-five without too many problems. It might take a while, but if you are in reasonable health and don't mind killing most of a day riding—and then a day or two to recover—you could actually ride a bike that far and not die from the attempt.

At least as long as there were no real mountains on the route.

But, as with life, when the road turns upward, when the steep climbs come, that is when you find out what you are really made of, and not until.

I will never forget my first attempt at climbing a road with an 8 percent grade. Not only was it at 8 percent, but the darn thing goes on for four miles too. I had been on lots of smaller climbs before that day, and I had only been afraid of dying on most of them, but after the first half mile of that beast I knew that my time was at hand and that my wife would be a widow and my children would end up fatherless before day's end. It's really only a mild exaggeration to say it that way too—I honestly did not know if I was going to be able to get to the top. My legs were burning, my eyes were stinging from the sweat, and my lungs felt as if the oxygen level in the beautiful mountain air had suddenly been reduced by about 75 percent. No matter how hard I tried, it seemed I could not get enough oxygen into my lungs to keep turning the pedals over.

I must have stopped a half a dozen times to catch my breath and give my poor legs a break, but because I kept starting again after every stop I was finally able to get to the top of that monster.

But here is the real kicker from that day: what I just described for you happened in the first twenty-five miles of a one hundred–mile day. Once I got to the top, we descended down the other side and spent the next three hours riding around the valley below, which only got us back to the base of what we had come down earlier that morning. Yes, that meant that to get back to the car I had to do another major climb with *really* exhausted legs. That side of the mountain is *only* a 7 percent grade, but it goes on for an extra mile. By the time I got back to the top and had gone down into the valley we started from, I was so exhausted that I cut fifteen miles out of the ride and only did eighty-five miles for the day.

Okay, so sanity is not a requirement to be a cyclist.

And yes, you can always make the argument that I brought it on myself. But since we are using my riding as a direct analogy to your life here, are you really sure you want to raise that question?

That experience happened eight years ago, and while I will never be a fast climber, I am now to the point that I'm not overly intimidated by anything up to 8 percent. Unless it goes on for more than five miles, or I am expected to maintain someone else's pace all the way to the top. As long as I can ride at my own pace—think old and slow here—I can now climb 8 percent grades without undue suffering. Notice I didn't say it is easy, only that I am no longer afraid of it killing me.

But then again, as it is in real life, there are roads steeper than 8 percent out there in the world. So my goal now is to get to the point that I can get up the 10 percent ramps in our area the way that I now do the 8 percent grades on the lower part of the mountain. For me, there is something very satisfying about the challenge of increasing my capacity to climb, and there is only one way to do that.

It isn't hard to figure out at all because it's just like living life. All I have to do is find the steep stuff and then just keep going. If I use all of my past experience to prepare for the attempt, if I am willing to put in the time doing the kind of training I know is required, I am pretty much guaranteed a successful day. It may take a while, and it may be a little painful on the way up, but I'll get to the top somehow.

But please never forget that my definition of riding success applies only to me, for almost any racer would just laugh at my meager efforts. But there is a far greater number of people who are amazed at what I can accomplish with my fifty-year-old body.

And there is one last comparison that I think might help expand the point involved here.

There are very few athletes in the world who are better known than Lance Armstrong. Even if he had won seven Tours de France without his experience with cancer it would still be one of the great achievements in sporting history. But after surviving a severe bout with cancer, his is a story that can only be described as stranger than fiction. If someone had written it as a book or screenplay beforehand, they would have been laughed out of every publishing and production office in the world.

So here is the best comparison I can give you between Lance Armstrong and myself: At its most basic level, cycling is about how much power a rider can produce and for how long a period of time that output can be maintained. Because of the technology available in today's world it is very easy to measure a rider's power output, which is then very valuable in determining what kind of workouts are needed to improve on this most basic of fitness requirements. (Note of clarification: power means electrical power, so think of generating the electricity required to power a one hundred–watt bulb as a comparison.)

To this point in time my maximum power output has been measured at a little over 350 watts, and I was able to maintain that level of output for a little over thirty seconds.

How does that compare to Lance Armstrong, you ask?

When he was in his final preparations to race another Tour de France, Lance was able to maintain a power output of four hundred watts for a little over an hour. As a comparison of speed, when on flat ground and with limited wind, that means that I can maintain a speed of twenty-four to twenty-six miles per hour for around eighteen minutes. After that kind of an effort, it takes almost five minutes before my lungs feel like they are getting enough air, and my legs will feel the effort for at least twenty-four hours.

At my strongest, and then only when riding in a paceline with stronger riders to pull me along, I have been able to maintain speeds over thirty miles an hour for maybe six to eight minutes. On multiple occasions, while under race conditions and riding by himself with no one to draft off of, Lance has maintained speeds of over thirty miles an hour for almost an hour and fifteen minutes.

Now, here is the more important comparison: in my opinion, the physical differences I have just described to you are an exact parallel of the spiritual differences between President Gordon B. Hinckley and myself.

What the differences mean

By now I hope the idea that everything is relative has dawned brightly in your mind.

Why am I able to climb an 8 percent grade on my bike without feeling like I'm going to die? Because I've done it many times now. Why am I able to have so much empathy for those who deal with some of life's toughest challenges? Because we have been forced to deal with some of the toughest challenges for the better part of a decade now.

But I didn't know how to deal with any of them until I was actually confronted with the need to do so. So, in the exact same way that my physical legs have improved their climbing strength and overall conditioning, my spiritual muscles and perspective have been strengthened by the trials and challenges that have come our way.

And in the exact same way that I seek out steeper mountains to climb on my bicycle, I am convinced that I asked Father in Heaven for some steep mountains to climb as a major part of my mortal experience. In the past few years I have not always been sure that I was grateful for the steepness of the road, but as time passes and we start to see some positive changes in our children's lives, I can honestly say that I would not trade what I have learned from this path for one with fewer challenges.

Well, that is enough cycling for now, but be assured that there will be other analogies that will come from that world in future chapters, for there are many more ways that life and riding a bike are direct parallels.

But we now have enough of a foundation in place to move on to the heart of the matter.

Principle Three

"As He Thinketh in His Heart, So Is He"—That's Not *Just the Way You Are*

3.1 Challenges and Choices

EVERYTHING THAT FOLLOWS FOR THE REST OF THIS book needs to be prefaced by a brief word of warning. In all my years of teaching the gospel I have always said that whenever I stand in front of a class I have three goals in mind:

First, I try to keep everyone awake. Don't laugh; I'm serious. And I am pleased to say that I have never had anyone fall asleep during one of my classes.

Second, I try to make people think. Now, I don't mean make them think a little bit; I mean make them think a whole lot. I mean get them to seriously consider how they feel about what is being said, whether they agree with it or not. I'm also trying to get them to examine why they do what they do or think how they do. In short, I'm really trying to challenge people's current thinking and understanding, which leads to goal number three.

Third, I try to motivate people to go home and read from the scriptures. We would all be much better off if we spent a lot more time with the scriptures and a whole lot less time with TV and the Internet.

If you have made it this far, I hope there have been at least a couple of things that have made you stop and think a bit about your current understanding or approach to life and its challenges. So far we have been dealing with doctrinal concepts and the impact that they have on our lives, but from here on things are going to get a lot more personal, for both of us. So this is just a fair warning that from here on we will be dealing with ideas that are much more personal in nature—and they will be dealt with in a manner that will hopefully make you think long and hard about why you think, do, believe, and say the things you do.

How we react to our challenges—all of us, not just me

As the challenges we have faced with our children have multiplied over a period of several years now, there have been many times when I have been asked how things were going at home. When that has happened I have tried to be appropriately honest, without being too specific as to what was going on or which of our children might be involved in a particular incident or behavior. There have also been times when someone has expressed their concern and been genuinely interested in a more detailed explanation of what we have been faced with. As you might guess from what has been mentioned already, the reactions to any of these conversations have ranged from shock to horror, from fear to amazement.

In virtually every instance, I have heard some variation of two different responses. Those being either "How have you done it?" or "I could never survive something like that."

Those responses are one of the major reasons for writing this book, and this chapter is where we will start to define the specific answers to those questions.

As of the summer of 2006, when I am writing this book, Linda and I have been married for twenty-seven and a half years and our children's major behavioral issues have been going on for nine years now. Yet it takes less than two hands to count the number of times that we have even raised our voices at each other in that time, let alone had some kind of major conflict over what might have been happening. It's not that we haven't had our disagreements, just that we have chosen to deal with them more quietly than seems to be the norm in the world today.

Two approaches to any issue

In every situation we encounter during this grand adventure called life, it is common for people to believe that there are but two distinct and totally separate approaches available to help us in dealing with our challenges:

1. We can choose to base our attitudes and thinking on the Atonement of Jesus Christ and the eternal truths of the revealed gospel.

2. We can choose to base our attitudes and thinking on the knowledge and standards of the world.

But as mentioned back in our foundation principles, I find this mutually exclusive approach to be based on shortsightedness, limited understanding, and false doctrine. For while it is plainly obvious that it is *always* best to base our thinking about any issue on the Lord and his revealed truth, we must once again acknowledge that the learning of man also provides a great deal of information that can be extremely helpful in the process. These two approaches actually become one and the same when we again state that any truth—meaning anything that is pure and unchangeable, *regardless of its source*, is profitable for the learning and edification of man.

And those thoughts should make it obvious that the best approach to the challenges of life is actually to combine the two.

I choose to do this because it allows me to keep both approaches in mind as I deal with my life and all of the different challenges that come my way. In using this dual approach, I find that my first thoughts are almost always gospel-centered, and then I supplement those understandings with things learned from other sources. And with those thoughts in mind, the chapters you have already read are the foundations that my thinking about life in general, and my thoughts about our challenges in particular, are built upon.

So you already have the spiritual foundations on which this approach to our challenges is based, but now we are going to add in some of the other ideas that have been used.

Attitude, perspective, and your right to choose

As we talked about back in the chapters of Principle One, Father is and must be no respecter of persons, meaning that regardless of our circumstances he loves each of us equally and will reward each of us in the same way if we will but keep the commandment attached to the desired reward.

But if Father loves us equally and always rewards us according to how well we keep his commandments, why does is it seem to be so difficult for us to take him at his word and move toward the positive results that are promised?

It is my firm conviction that once we have a proper understanding of our relationship with God, the only things that can ever hold us back are *self-imposed* limits. After all, if we do in fact have the ability to someday become as God now is, if our eternal Father finds his greatest glory in our improvement and progress, is it not plainly obvious that the weakness is in our attitudes and perspectives and not in his willingness to support us in our efforts?

And so the realization must then be that nothing, absolutely nothing—including genetics—has a bigger impact on your life and on your ability to gain favor with God than what you allow yourself to think, feel, and believe about yourself.

If that statement is a little too bold for you, then please refer to Proverbs 23:7: "As he thinketh in his heart, so is he."

Yes, I realize that what you have just read is pretty controversial to a large cross section of people, and in this case I'm not just playing devil's advocate to try to get you to think about what you believe. I am also not saying that genetics aren't involved in determining some of the characteristics of our personalities and lives; there is no question that they play a significant part in the development of your personality and approach to life. But nothing involved in the process of your development has a greater impact on who you are, what you believe, and what you become than the pictures, sounds, and feelings—all of the thoughts—that you *allow* to play out across the stage of your own mind.

For a further explanation of these concepts, please consider the following comments from one of the more remarkable talks ever given by President Boyd K. Packer. Early in the talk he quotes the following from his own patriarchal blessing: "You have been given a body of such physical proportions and fitness as to enable your spirit to function through it unhampered by physical impediments. You should cherish this as a great heritage. Guard and protect it—take nothing into it that shall harm the organs thereof because it is sacred. *It is the instrument of your mind and the foundation of your character.*"[1]

He then makes this very powerful statement: "I found that it did not matter, really, what kind of bodies we have, so long as we understand that our spirit and our body are combined in such a way that *our body becomes an instrument of our mind* and the foundation of our character."

Later in the talk, he quotes D&C 93:30–31: "All truth is independent in that sphere in which God has placed it, to act for itself, as all intelligence also; *otherwise there is no existence.* Behold, here is the agency of man." President Packer then continued, "So there we are. We have agency. *What happens in our lives and in our pattern of eternal progression is just what we decide it will be.*"[2]

As a final example of the accuracy of these statements, please consider this question: If my spirit were to leave my body, would my body be able to feel anything at all?

And no, that is not a trick question. It is simply a question designed to help you recognize the fact that without the presence of a spirit, our bodies are incapable of *feeling* anything at all. This should help clarify the great eternal truth that our bodies truly are the instruments of our minds. This leads us to another of the great lies in all of eternity. It's not the spirit and mind that are willing and the flesh that is weak, but actually the other way around. For if the body cannot feel or do anything without the presence of a spirit, that must mean that it will *only* do what the mind and spirit require of it, or what they allow it to do, and nothing more.

And here is an example of how the learning of man supports the spiritual principles just explained.

A story is told about twin boys who were born into very difficult circumstances. Their father was an alcoholic who abused them physically, verbally, and emotionally throughout their childhoods. As they grew older and began to think more and more for themselves, one followed in virtually every one of their father's footsteps, while the other was the exact opposite in almost every way.

Where the first started drinking heavily at a young age, the other drank only in the most moderate of amounts. When the first was abusive and unkind to other children or small animals, the other was a model of kindness and courtesy. As the first followed his father into a life of menial jobs and financial misery, the second completed college and was successful and prosperous in comparison. Son number one was never able to successfully maintain a relationship with a woman and never married, while son number two had a very loving wife and beautiful children of his own.

These two men were identical—*there was no genetic difference between them whatsoever*—and they were raised in exactly the same home and circumstances, yet their lives were as opposite as they could have possibly been.

How is such a thing possible? When their stories became known and their lives were being compared and studied, the people conducting the study asked both of them the same question. Yes, we are back to Why? again. In this case, the question was, "Why are you the way you are?"

To their amazement they got the exact same answer from both men. Remember, we are talking about genetically-identical twins here; it shouldn't be that big of a surprise. Their answer was, "With him [meaning their father] for an example, what else could I have been?"

In all my years of studying the importance of attitude and perspective upon the human condition, I have never found a better way of making the point than that little story. It covers all the bases of comparison in that the genetic makeup of the men is identical, they were raised in the same home and circumstances, and they gave the exact same answer to the most important question of their lives—why are you the way you are?

So given the fact that the circumstances of their youth were identical in every way, the *only* thing that made any difference in their lives was the attitudes and perspectives that each took from the lessons of his individual life.

And in the exact same fashion, you take the experiences that make up your life and place them in the context that makes the most sense to you. You do this by assigning feelings, emotions, and reactions to everything you have ever experienced, and those feelings, emotions, and reactions are the tools that you then use to turn your experiences into the thoughts, attitudes, and actions that make up your life.

So, to put a bit finer point on it, you are not "just the way you are," you are the way you are because you *chose* to be that way, and you chose to be that way because all of your accumulated experience has brought you to that point. Your experiences have brought you to the point that you know how to be the way you are, which is just a fancy way of saying that you had to *learn* how to be the way you are. And the reason you stay that way is that those thoughts, attitudes, and actions are what you have allowed yourself to become comfortable with.

(Just a quick housekeeping note here: a few pages back I told you that I prefer to start any learning process with the spiritual principle involved and then add in the things that come from other sources. In this case, and because this concept is so critical to everything that follows, we will continue with the reasoned approach to this topic and then add some additional doctrinal examples. I don't want you to think I have abandoned my own logic, but I also think you will recognize why the sequence is better this way. And once again, back to your regularly scheduled programming.)

Notes

1. Boyd K. Packer, "The Instrument of Your Mind and the Foundation of Your Character" (CES fireside, Brigham Young University, Provo, UT, Feb. 2, 2003); italics added.
2. Ibid.

3.2 How We Learn Things

IN THE LAST CHAPTER, WE WORKED TO ESTABLISH THE fact that our behavior is based on specific choices that we make, and we had to learn how to make those choices in the first place. But why is the fact that we have to learn to be the way we are so critical to the subject, you ask? (Come on . . . ask yourself the question. It makes the whole process much easier.)

Because—and this is another very critical concept for you to gain an understanding of—*if you can figure out how you learned to do something the way you do, that means you can also learn how to do it differently.*

Most of us have never even considered the idea that we can actually figure out how we learned to do any of the things that we do, which makes it a pretty big shift in our thinking just to consider such a thought. If we are serious about gaining that kind of increased ability, it means that we need to understand how we learn things in the first place.

It has long been established that the vast majority of us are born with five senses, and that we use those senses to gather, observe, filter, and process all of the information that comes our way during the course of our lives. Those senses are sight, sound, smell, taste, and touch, or what are more accurately described as tactile sensations and feelings.

From that list it shouldn't be too much of a stretch to recognize that our senses are the tools we use to record and then create our impressions of and reactions to every experience that we ever have. So, starting with our initial womb-based awareness of sights, sounds, and sensations, the miracle that is the human brain begins an ongoing recording of everything we ever see, hear, smell, taste, touch, and feel for our entire lives. Think for just a second about the magnitude of that statement. Literally *everything* you have ever experienced is recorded right there in you own brain, and not just recorded as part of some separate system or device; it is actually a part of you, a fully integrated system—and you are the only person alive who knows exactly how yours works. After all, you're the only one living in your own head, so you have to be the only one who knows exactly how yours works.

So let's talk about the process a bit. As stated above, all five of your senses are a part of the ongoing recording that is being made by your brain, but since that idea is a bit much for me, I like to think of it as a multi-track recorder with one track for each sense. That idea makes it a little easier for me to get my own brain around the concept.

So, virtually all of the waking records will contain at least pictures—either movies or stills—and sound. Then when I walk into the kitchen while my wife is cooking dinner, smell is added to the record. And when I actually put the first bite of food into my mouth, taste is also added. But touch is more difficult to describe because while it includes our kinesthetic senses, meaning that we can tell the difference between hard and soft, it also includes all of the feelings that come from your thoughts about the sensory input described above. So what we are talking about are the specific thinking processes that you go through, individually, to generate the thoughts, feelings, and emotions that you do.

And right about now you are probably thinking that that's enough technical psychology. How about a few understandable examples?

When did you learn the difference between a cat and a dog? Exactly when and how did you learn to recognize that even though they both have four legs, two eyes, two ears, a tail, and fur, there is a fundamental difference between a cat and a dog? Who told you what the difference was? Who decided that the one that barks would be called a dog and the one that purrs would be called a cat? And who ever had enough power to decide that the letters C-A-T would designate the one and the letters D-O-G would be the other? (And yes, I know about Adam and his naming everything, but you get the point.)

But here is the even more interesting part of the process: when you see the letters D-O-G, or when you look at either a picture of a dog or an actual dog, what is the specific process you go through—in the privacy of your own head—that gets you to the point that you can say with such absolute surety that that animal, or those three letters, refer to your favorite pet? And do you see the dog you are looking at and then compare that image to the first time you ever saw a dog, or do you hear it bark first and then see that first picture?

When do the feelings of love and appreciation for that most loyal of all pets come into your awareness? Is it when you hear the new dog bark and associate that sound back to the pictures of the dog you had as a child, or do those feelings wait until you are wrestling and playing with this new animal? And when do those same feelings become associated directly to this animal instead of needing the split-second refresher reference to the original one?

Are you smiling yet?

After reading those few paragraphs, are you starting to realize that there is a lot more happening in your thought patterns than you have ever considered before? I hope that the concept of *relational thinking*—the process of combining the input from all five senses to define the meaning of a specific experience—is also becoming clearer to you. To further illustrate the concept, here is a different approach to the subject. I found this in my email inbox one day, and I like it because it puts the idea of repeatable patterns into a framework that may be more understandable to some, especially those who are a little younger and may have spent some time playing video games.

> "Enemies move in predictable patterns."
>
> It sent chills down my spine as I saw the statement. I saw the deep revelation behind it, the awesome truth. Did I read this in some deep spiritual document? Did I hear it from some wise master? Did I glean this from the strategies of some great general?
>
> No. I saw it on a billboard. The billboard was advertising video game awards. I guess it meant that all video games have repeatable and thus predictable patterns. If you could figure out the pattern, you had a better chance of winning.
>
> *Enemies move in predictable patterns.* I immediately saw this as a great truth in life. The vast majority of things that we struggle with, we have struggled with before. It's not new. It repeats. It's old and familiar stuff. It's a predictable pattern. I can't think of any new flaws that I have. I can't think of any behavior that I want to change now that I didn't have ten years ago.
>
> All of my enemies move in predictable patterns.
>
> I struggle with diet, trying to eat healthy and moderately.

> I struggle with pride, trying to have enough humility to hear God, enough self-assurance to do what God wants me to do and then not get puffed up about it when he gives me success.
>
> I struggle with budgeting money.
>
> I struggle with spending enough time studying.
>
> I struggle with spending enough quality time with the kids, my wife, and others who need my help.
>
> I struggle with looking and thinking where I shouldn't.
>
> I struggle with just not wanting to do what needs to be done.
>
> I struggle with enemies, enemies that rob me of so much that the Creator desires for me.
>
> All of these enemies have been with me for a long time. If you are honest with yourself, you have them too, enemies that move in predictable patterns. Those who win at the game figure out the *pattern* of the enemy and *break* it.

Do these simple comments help you to begin to understand the power of the concept? Are you beginning to realize that you really did have to learn to be the way you are? Are you intrigued by the idea that if you can figure out how you do something now—meaning the specific process you go through to access a particular feeling or emotion—it might just make it easier to change that process and move towards a healthier and more fulfilling approach to your life?

If not, don't despair. We are still very early in the process of explaining how these things work, and you didn't get to be the way you are overnight either.

Why information matters

Now then, here is another very critical thing for you to learn about the relationship between thoughts, feelings, emotions, and behavior. It is that your thoughts *always* precede your feelings, emotions, and behavior. Yes, it may only be by a matter of nanoseconds, but that does not change the fact that your thoughts always come first.

And why is this truth so important for us to understand?

Because if you recognize that every feeling or emotion you ever experience is preceded by a thought—meaning one of those repeatable patterns described above—it should crystallize in your mind the great truth that you have far more control over your feelings, emotions, and behaviors than you may have ever dreamed of before right now.

So, here is the sequence involved in the thinking that precedes any behavior:

- Sensory input—all five senses worth.
- Association to a previous experience by comparing new input to old—defined here as *relational thinking*.
- Thinking about and then choosing a response. Remember that your possible responses are based on how you feel about the thoughts that you start with.
- Emotions and responses/actions, which are a result of the intensity of the feelings that are chosen in the thinking process.

So, what do you have to do to get a different response to almost any given situation? This may sound drastically oversimplified, but all that is required is for you to learn to slow your reaction process enough—in other words, teach yourself to take a split second to consider more than just your initial, usually very emotional, reaction to any given situation—it will virtually guarantee that your reactions are more appropriate to each specific situation, and less emotionally charged too.

Isn't the single biggest issue involved in interpersonal communication the problems that are created when we speak first and think later? And isn't it also a universal truth that when we reflect on our past behavior, we are frequently embarrassed by comments that are based on those initial emotional reactions? Yet when we take the time to give a more considered and rational response, those types of problems seldom come up.

This just proves the point that we already have these more appropriate reactions available to us; for if we didn't already have them within us we could not even come up with them upon a longer and less emotional reflection. So what we really need is just a little more time to bring them to the forefront of our thinking.

Then once you have taught yourself how to consider at least two options before reacting, think of how much more situation-specific your reactions will be if you learn to consider four or five different responses before opening your mouth.

And here is a different kind of example about how the information available (the thoughts that you consider as possible responses to a particular experience) can have a dramatic impact on how you think, feel, and choose to react to that experience.

For this example to mean anything at all it has to be about something that happens to you. So there you are, at a street corner on your way to a job interview. This is an interview with a company that you have been interested in working with for quite a while, and you are excited about the opportunity now in front of you. This really is your dream job. You have dressed in the best clothes that you have for this very important occasion and done everything that you know how to do to make a good impression in those critical first few seconds of the interview.

Did I mention that it was raining pretty hard about half an hour ago and that even though the rain has stopped, there is quite a bit of water still standing in the gutters?

Yes, you guessed it. As you stand at the corner waiting for the light to change, a truck suddenly swerves toward the curb and drenches you in water and muck. In the initial fraction of a second that it takes for your brain to confirm what has just happened, you are instantly enraged by what you assume to be the intentional actions of the driver. You *know* that he had to have taken this action just to destroy your life and ruin the opportunity for you to get your dream job.

How long did it take for you to get to that reaction? Not more than two or three seconds—and probably quite a bit less time than that.

You sputter and yell at the truck as it pulls away, and that goes on for a few seconds before you suddenly notice the young mother standing in the middle of the intersection crying hysterically. Only after another few seconds of observing what is going on do you realize that the truck's driver had no intention of ruining your day at all, and that in fact he had swerved to avoid the three-year-old little girl who had wandered into the intersection and is only now being held safely in her terrified mother's arms.

How long did it take for you to go from feeling complete rage at the driver to feeling intense gratitude that the life of the little girl had been spared? And when you realized that your discomfort was a small price to pay for the life of a little girl, how did you feel about your reaction toward the truck driver?

As defined above, and expanded upon by this example, how many times in your life have you reacted too quickly to a situation, and then when more information became available have either been embarrassed by your actions or have actually had to apologize for what you said or did. You know, how many times have you had to eat a little bit of crow?

I hope all of this helps you begin to understand not only the speed with which your reactions can happen, but also the fact that those reactions can have some pretty extreme effects based on two simple things—more information and more time.

Back to "just the way I am"—the spiritual side

For a very long time now I have been both mildly amused and mightily frustrated whenever I hear someone trot out the old line "That's just the way I am." How many times have you said it yourself?

I am mildly amused because it gives so much insight into the thinking and mind-set of the person making the comment. They seem to be saying, "Don't bother me with more information or a perspective that might require some work or effort on my part. I'm very comfortable where I am with my thinking, and I don't want to do much more of it."

A good friend of mine has a T-shirt that reads, "The only difference between a rut and a grave is dimension." I find that there is great clarity in that thought, and I am afraid that a great many of us are in an emotional and intellectual grave without even realizing it.

On the other hand, my frustration comes from the fact that there are so many highly religious people who make that excuse. Please note that I did not specify which religion, just that there are lots of religious people who make that statement. It really doesn't matter what religion is involved, because virtually every religion on earth has the improvement of the individual at the core of its teachings. Then when you get to the Judeo-Christian religions—where *everything* that the prophets teach about the Messiah revolves around the process of repentance and personal improvement—it gets even more interesting.

Have you ever recognized that there is a direct contradiction between saying you believe in the Messiah and all of his teachings, and then saying, "That's just the way I am"?

Have you ever noticed the statement that usually precedes that one (you know, "I didn't have a choice") for what it really is? Or do you just not recognize the fact that when you make these statements you are giving away your own agency? What you are in fact saying is, "I am not willing to examine my thoughts and actions closely enough to find out if I need to do something differently."

There's a real dichotomy in saying that you believe in Jesus Christ and his teachings and then trying to take the position of "That's just the way I am," for isn't the doctrine of repentance simply the process of evaluating your own life to discover where the improvements are needed? And isn't that process the polar opposite of the concept behind "Leave me alone; that's just the way I am"?

For me personally, those words—"That's just the way I am"—stick in my throat the same way that it was impossible for Fonzie of *Happy Days* fame to ever say that he was wrong. Do you remember how funny it was to watch Henry Winkler stammer and stutter on the *wro* . . . part of the word? He simply couldn't bring himself to admit that he ever made a mistake, and it turned into one of the classic comedy bits in TV history.

Unfortunately, it isn't quite as funny when applied in this context. Sorry for the downer.

After reading the chapters under the first two principle headings of this book, I hope those statements don't have quite as much sting to them as they might have had before, and I certainly hope they do not offend you. But I also hope that they ring a little more true for you now than they did before. I hope you are starting to come to the realization that it must be that way, that Father did not create you one way or another in regards to *any* of the specifics of your life, because—yes, here it comes again—to do so would take away your agency and eliminate both your opportunity to learn by your own experience and your accountability before the laws that govern all of creation.

So, there it is in a nutshell—a very brief description of the processes that make you who and what you are.

3.3 Producing Your Own Life

IT HAS BEEN MY EXPERIENCE THAT THERE IS A LOT OF great information available from both the spiritual and mortal sides of the equation about what makes us who and what we are, but practical application is another matter entirely. So the rest of the information under this principle heading will deal with different ways to apply what we have discussed thus far.

We begin with two examples of different approaches that can be used to deal with specific challenges in our lives. The first showed up in my email a while back, and I kept it because I liked the approach this man took to some very difficult challenges. The second defines an even more specific approach that I have used in my own life. Here is the first one:

> John was the kind of guy you love to hate. He was always in a good mood and always had something positive to say. When someone would ask him how he was doing, he would reply, "If I were any better, I would be twins!"
>
> He was a natural motivator.
>
> If an employee was having a bad day, John was there telling the employee how to look on the positive side of the situation.
>
> Seeing this style really made me curious, so one day I went up and said, "I don't get it. You can't be a positive person all of the time. How do you do it?"
>
> He replied, "Each morning I wake up and say to myself, you have two choices today. You can choose to be in a good mood, or, you can choose to be in a bad mood. I choose to be in a good mood.
>
> "Each time something bad happens I can choose to be a victim, or I can choose to learn from it. I choose to learn from it.

"Every time someone comes to me complaining, I can choose to accept their complaining, or I can point out the positive side of life. I choose the positive side of life."

"Yeah, right. It's not that easy," I protested.

"Yes, it is," he said. "Life is all about choices. When you cut away all the junk, every situation is a choice. You choose how you react to situations. You choose how people affect your mood. You choose to be in a good mood or bad mood. The bottom line: It's your choice how you live your life."

I reflected on what he said. Soon thereafter I quit my job to start my own business. We lost touch, but I often thought about him when I made a choice about life instead of reacting to it.

Several years later I heard that he was involved in a serious accident, falling some sixty feet from a communications tower. After eighteen hours of surgery and weeks of intensive care, he was released from the hospital with rods placed in his back.

I saw him about six months after the accident. When I asked him how he was, he replied, "If I were any better, I'd be twins. Wanna see my scars?"

I declined to see his wounds, but I did ask him what had gone through his mind as the accident took place.

"The first thing that went through my mind was the well-being of my soon-to-be born daughter," he replied. "Then, as I lay on the ground, I remembered that I had two choices: I could choose to live or . . . I could choose to die. I chose to live."

"Weren't you scared? Did you lose consciousness?" I asked.

He continued, "The paramedics were great. They kept telling me I was going to be fine. But when they wheeled me into the ER and I saw the expressions on the faces of the doctors and nurses, I got really scared. In their eyes I read, 'He's a dead man.' I knew I needed to take action."

"What did you do?" I asked.

"Well, there was a big burly nurse shouting questions at me," said John. "She asked if I was allergic to anything. 'Yes,' I replied. The doctors and nurses stopped working as they waited for my reply.

"I took a deep breath and yelled, 'Gravity.' Over their laughter I told them, 'I am choosing to live. Operate on me as if I am alive, not dead.' "

He lived, thanks to the skill of his doctors, but also because of his amazing attitude. I learned from him that every day we have the choice to live fully. *Attitude, after all, is everything.*

"Take therefore no thought for the morrow: for the morrow shall take thought for the things of itself. Sufficient unto the day is the evil thereof"

(Matthew 6:34). After all, today is the tomorrow you worried about yesterday.

Now then, this second example comes from my own life, but it also needs a little more of a setup than the first.

As part of the treatment program that one of our children is currently involved with we have been exposed to what I like to call Statements of Truth. One of them says, "Childhood is a combination of adventures and abuses."

Well duh, that's the nature of the parent-child relationship.

All of us have a large number of both, and most adults in today's world also realize that how their parents interacted with them has a significant impact on how they feel about themselves and how they approach life. I have quite a few of those kinds of experiences, and the most powerful ones involve my father.

For a very long time whenever I felt insecure about something or was unsure about what to do or think, I repeated a thinking pattern of falling back on feelings and memories of my father telling me that I never followed through on anything or that I never finished an assigned task properly or that I was lazy or that I would never amount to anything or . . . you get the picture.

A good percentage of those things happened before I was ten years old, and because they were repeated with great regularity and emotional emphasis, I believed them. After all, he was my father, and every little boy just knows that his dad is the smartest, strongest, best dad in the whole world. So when those things were said over and over again with great vocal emphasis, they were then turned into feelings in my brain—and it was only natural for me to buy into them completely.

So no matter how much he loved me, without knowing he was doing it—and certainly without any intent of doing so—my dad imbedded some less than desirable messages in my very impressionable brain. And from there, as all of us do to one degree or another, I then turned them into some very unpleasant thoughts and feelings about myself.

It's been quite a few years now since I decided I needed a better way to represent those experiences, but I needed to do this so that I could get away from a good many of the negative feelings that I used to have about myself.

Maybe you're thinking, *But wait a minute, how can you change those things? Your dad said them and you believed them, so—that's just the way you are.*

But then you remember, *It's my brain; my body becomes an instrument of my mind, so it's my life. Heavenly Father said, "Power is in them and they are agents unto themselves," which means that I am under no obligation to accept bad information or messages, regardless of who they come from or how good or bad their intentions may have been.*

What follows next is a description of one of the more successful approaches that I have used to change the way I react to those inappropriate messages.

First of all, you need to think of the Disney movie *The Sword and the Stone.* In the movie there is a wizard's duel in which Merlin and an old witch named Madame Mim start turning themselves into all sorts of weird creatures to try to gain an advantage over the other. At one point Madam Mim turns herself into a big green dragon with a huge belly and tiny little wings, but you still see her head on the dragon body. Then the she gets purple spots that move all around the body and face, which make her look very funny.

Well, when I realized that my internal representation of my dad was getting in my face, just like he did when I was a kid, I decided it was time to change that picture and find out if a different picture would get a different reaction. My first step in doing this was to turn my internal picture of him into the dragon from the magical duel in the movie. Then, just like in the movie, I put his head on the dragon's body—which, to me, was pretty funny all by itself—and then I added the purple spots and watched him bounce all around and get really upset because of what I was doing to him.

Then I found that if I really wanted to feel differently about things, all I had to do was speed up the sound of his voice to somewhere between Alvin the Chipmunk and my dad's normal voice on helium. It's all animated—except for his face, which is three dimensional and very real looking—and when I made all of those changes it completely changed my reaction and how I was feeling about what he was saying to me.

When I first started using this approach it wasn't usually until I changed the voice that I really cracked up and started laughing, but I've done it so many times that if I need to do it now I'm usually chuckling as soon as the head goes on the dragon. If I take it all the way to changing the voice, it's usually because I'm explaining it to someone else the same way I just did for you.

But the real magic of this approach isn't in the specific pictures and sounds that I use to change my emotional reactions to my father's messages; it's in the process itself. The critical point here—and it is impossible to overstate how vital this really is—is that by taking control of the pictures and sounds that we allow to play out across the stage of our mind, by taking conscious control of the things that we allow ourselves to see and hear, we can completely change our reactions, feelings, and emotions related to any of the events and experiences of our lives.

Thus, "As he thinketh in his heart, so is he" is proven to be an absolute truth in the realms of both spiritual and worldly learning.

But how is all of that possible, you ask?

Remember how we talked about associating pictures and sounds with feelings and emotions to create a repeatable pattern? That is all that the process I have just described is really about. So when I learned these concepts almost twenty years ago and first created my little movie, I ran it enough times that whenever my brain—we're talking about my subconscious mind here—sees or hears any of the unpleasant stuff from my dad, it automatically starts to run the new movie. Therefore, the old reactions never get a chance to even get started, which means that I now feel very differently about myself.

As it was said in the first story, "Yeah, right. It's not that easy." You think to yourself, *I could never do that. I could never figure out how to do something like that with my own brain.* But I assure you that you can. All it takes is enough honesty and self-awareness to examine your current approaches to life and the challenges it brings, and then making the commitment to putting in a little effort and practice. You know, start figuring out how your own brain runs now, and then change the things that you don't like.

Is it just me, or does that sound an awful lot like the repentance process too?

I have been doing this for long enough now that I have actually been asked on several occasions, "Do you ever have a bad day?" My response is usually something along the line of, "Oh yes, I have lots of them. But that doesn't mean that you need to know about them."

But here is the real question: Are you ready for something that drastic in your own life? Are you ready to take that much control of your own brain and use it in a way that will bring more peace and contentment into your life, or are you going to continue falling back on "Leave me alone; that's just the way I am"?

After all, it's your agency—it really is your God-given right to make decisions for yourself, and that can only mean that those decisions are completely up to you.

And at this point I also hope you realize that one of the greatest benefits of this approach is that it makes it possible for you to stop worrying about what someone said in the past. After a very short period of time you will realize that you really are better equipped to manage your own brain than anyone else ever could be. It's not that you disregard others' opinions; it's just that with your new position of emotional strength—which can only come because of an increase in self-awareness and self-confidence—you are much better equipped to analyze and respond to what others say. This can only make your responses more rational and appropriate, and that idea can only bring us back to the concept of learning to give yourself more time to gather information so that your responses are more reasoned and less emotional.

A different kind of example

This next example comes from my wife. As part of our child's treatment program, every three weeks or so we get to have a family counseling session. We had one of those sessions in early August of 2006. As you might guess from what you have already read about our children's escapades, there are lots of different things that need to be addressed and dealt with, and some of them are less than pleasant. All of our emotions can get pretty raw, and that's the kind of session we had that day.

On the way home Linda was thinking about what she could say, and how to best say it, to help our child better understand the real nature of the healing process. What follows is what came to her while she was driving down the freeway. You can judge for yourself how well she did and what the source of her idea is, but I have no question at all that it came directly from the Lord.

Linda received these inspired words to say to our child:

> As I was leaving the building today I felt I needed to express to you that the things that happened in your past are not who you are. They are not your heart or your spirit. I want for you to be able to put away the shame you feel and to recognize how precious you

are. Some thoughts came to me that I would like to share with you that I hope might help. So, here is my analogy.

The choices you have made are like clothes. They are not you, or who you are inside your heart and spirit. They are like an outfit that you put on and wore for a while. This outfit was the popular thing to wear. You may have felt cool in it. Your friends liked you better when you wore it because they wore theirs too.

But when you look back on that outfit now, you start to realize some things.

You never really felt comfortable when you were wearing it, and you didn't realize that it didn't really fit you. You continued to wear it because you didn't realize you had anything else to wear.

You don't wear that outfit anymore. You have put it away in a drawer. You wear new clothes now, clothes that express your own style and personality.

As you look at old pictures of yourself wearing that outfit, you can say to yourself, "What was I thinking? I can't believe I ever liked that outfit." You may sometimes take that old outfit out of the drawer, hold it up, and look at it. You may think of all the reasons why you wore that old outfit in the past.

You don't like it anymore. You have grown in many ways since the last time you put that outfit on. It doesn't fit you at all now. So you put it back in the drawer where you have been keeping it. You close the drawer and walk away, wearing your beautiful new clothes.

Someday, when you are ready, you will take that old outfit out of the drawer and throw it away. As time goes by, you will not even remember that you wore it.

I hope this helps you to see what your dad and I see. The things that you still hold on to can be put away; they were never a part of you. We have always seen past the outfit to who you are inside.

We love you more than words can express.

Wear your new clothes proudly.

Needless to say, I am more than just a little proud of my dear wife, and after reading her words, you have just a glimpse of the insight and spirit that she brings into our lives. I am also in awe of her wisdom, and the very simple way she has of saying such monumentally profound things.

If I work really hard at it for the rest of my life, I may begin to approach having a very small portion of her goodness.

I have read this analogy several times now, and there are three things about it that stand out to me.

First, from a doctrinal standpoint, everything she says is completely sound. One of the most profound ideas that any of us will ever come in contact with is that what we do defines *what* we are, not *who* we are. It is true that what we do defines our character, and that it also gives a frighteningly accurate picture of how we think and feel about ourselves (we will talk in great detail about this item in the next chapter), but nothing we ever do can take away the fact that who we are is children of an all-loving Heavenly Father. Nothing we do can ever take away the fact that we have the right to lay claim to the Atonement of Jesus Christ. Further, Linda's analogy of our actions being like clothes that we can change is in complete harmony with the doctrine of repentance and personal improvement, and as such it is a wonderful metaphor for that process.

Second, from a psychological standpoint, everything she says is completely sound. Compare her analogy to my process of changing how I react to my father's messages from my youth. It should be pretty obvious how changing the pictures involved in her analogy would provide some very different, and much healthier, reactions for our child. Now transform your pictures of this analogy from involving drugs or alcohol to being about over-eating or over-reacting or over-whatever else that you might need to address. Try it in your own head and see if you don't feel very differently about that subject. I promise you that you will.

Third, from a therapeutic standpoint, her analogy is a masterpiece in providing reinforcement and help to a struggling teenager. (It would work for a person of any age though.) The nature of this analogy provided a great deal of personal freedom for our child to implement it in the ways that made the most sense individually. Those statements are also very respectful of the individuality of our child or anyone else who might like to use them, and respect for each of us as individuals is imperative in the therapeutic experience.

Further, some of the phrases from Linda's analogy are so powerful that they need some additional review and commentary, but there are other concepts that need to be put in place first, so let's move on again.

3.4 How Your Brain Works

AS HUMAN BEINGS, OUR LIST OF EMOTIONAL NEEDS IS very short, but the impact of whether or not those needs are met is enormous. A short list of our emotional needs would include

- Love and affection
- Acceptance and approval
- Security
- A sense of control and predictability
- A sense of accomplishment
- Pursuing pleasure and avoiding pain

And here is another of those very critical items for you to recognize and understand. No matter how negative the action, and no matter how incomprehensible the logic may be to someone else, literally every decision we ever make, and everything we ever do during our lives, is simply intended to meet one or more of these most basic needs.

And yes, I know that there are many valid arguments for expanding the list beyond the few items listed above, but it seems to me that if these six items are a regular part of our lives, then everything else can easily fall under one of these headings. But the real point here isn't to define the specific items on the list. The point is to get you thinking a little more about what motivates the thoughts, feelings, actions, and choices of your life.

We are now to the point in our discussion that there are two more key truths that must be brought to your attention. Among the most important and powerful truths you will ever learn about your brain and how it works is the fact that your subconscious mind cannot tell the difference between an actual experience, one that you live and breath your way through, and one that is vividly imagined.

Now just in case you think you misread that, here it is again so that there is no misunderstanding. *It is impossible for your subconscious mind to differentiate between a real-life experience and one that you vividly create within the confines of your own mind.*

The power of this concept lies in the fact that it exposes the critical nature of our inner dialogue, and when added to your new understanding about how to control that dialogue, it further demonstrates the amount of control that we have over our thoughts, feelings, and actions. And yes, I realize that we live in the Western world, where our concepts of mind-body harmony are not nearly as developed as they are in much of the Eastern world, but none of these things can change the eternal truth that we have a far greater degree of control over what we think, feel, and do than most of us will ever understand.

If you would like another graphic example of this truth, just refer to the sports industry, where a large percentage of elite level athletes work with some form of sports psychologist. Why is this such a good example you ask? Because in virtually every case, the psychologist has their client spend a significant amount of time vividly visualizing ever-greater successes in their particular sport.

Now why take any time at all to practice a physical skill without even moving a muscle? Why practice purely in the imagined world of your mind? Isn't it obvious that the only possible answer is that these professionals, both the psychologists and the athletes, know from their own experience that the brain cannot differentiate between a real experience and one that is vividly imagined? And so they truly know—again, from their own experience—that they can make almost as much progress using visualization as they can with actual physical practice.

Another example would be the use of biofeedback to learn how to control your heart rate or blood pressure. There are many cases where subjects are instructed to visualize sitting in a tub of cold water, and the subjects report feeling the same sensations they would if they were sitting in an actual tub. One of the body's normal reactions to such a situation is to slow down the heart rate and conserve energy to the most vital parts of the body, but there are thousands of people who can get the same reaction just by vividly imagining the cold.

Finally, what do you think of the idea of professional soldiers being taught to lower their heart rate so that they can shoot more accurately *between* heartbeats. How important do you think that skill might be on the battlefield? And just how important do you think that much self-awareness and self-control might be to you in your life?

Next up on our list of important truths to understand is the specific interaction between your conscious and subconscious minds. At some level, most of us already understand that our subconscious plays an enormous role in how we think, feel, and act, but the interaction between the two parts of our mind is far less understood. This lack of understanding is one of the great tragedies of our lives because it is the single most important key we have to regulating our feelings, emotions, and behavior.

This is because there is a distinct difference between how your conscious and subconscious mind process information. Your subconscious is the "always-on" part of your mind, in that it never sleeps or spaces out or takes a break of any kind. There are even examples of patients who have been able to recreate exact conversations that occurred between the operating room staff while a patient was sound asleep under general anesthesia.

So, because of its "always-on" status, your subconscious does not have time to analyze any of the content that it receives from your five senses; it just records everything and files all of it away for future reference. And here is the most important key to understanding the relationship between your conscious mind and your subconscious mind: your subconscious mind accepts everything your conscious mind tells it *without question*.

So every time my internal voice—or in my case, my father's voice inside my own head—told me that I was never good enough, every time I got the message that what mattered to me was unimportant, every time I felt like a failure, every time I . . . you get the message; my subconscious never questioned the messages it was being given. It simply accepted all of it as true, and then when a question or circumstance similar to the first one came along it reacted according to that truth—once again—without ever questioning the original reaction or the information that it was based on.

As many years have passed and my understanding of how my brain works has grown, I have come to realize that the meanings I created in my brain as a child were *not* the meanings that my father intended. I now realize that my father was doing the best job he knew how to do, and I also know that the same messages that I once interpreted as critical and harmful are in fact the greatest manifestations of his love that he ever gave me. Further, I am now grateful for those messages, and I honor and respect my father for doing the best job that he knew how to do.

And here is one final thought on these concepts and the power they can have in your life: if there is one human reaction that is more prevalent than "That's just the way I am," the only one I can think of is "I can't" or "I could never."

"I can't what?" or "I could never what?" you ask?

Anything you can come up with. It doesn't matter what the "I can't" statement is attached to; what you are really saying can only be one of two things. It has to be either "I don't know how to . . ." or "I won't even try."

Then under the heading of "words actually mean something," consider the fact that the word *can't* is a contraction of the words *can* and *not*. So when you say you can't, what you are really saying is "I can, but I am in the process of not doing it." The meaning of *won't* is even more obvious, for it is simply "I am unwilling to even try."

Now here is a very interesting and important question for you. When you were six months old, did you ever think to yourself, *I can't learn how to crawl* or *I can't learn how to walk* or *I can't* . . . anything? Do you realize that if you had, you would not be able to do any of those things today? But you didn't know any better then, so you went merrily on your way and learned how to do all sorts of things that if you had to learn now your self-limiting beliefs would kick in, and you would prevent yourself from gaining those skills. Or maybe that's what is happening in several areas of you life, and you just haven't had anyone point it out to you until right now.

Here are a few more basic examples, just to help solidify the point.

How easy would it be for you to learn a new language at this point in your life? What would it take for you to learn to play a musical instrument now? How do you feel about public speaking, and what would it take for you to be more comfortable with that experience?

Yet you not only learned a new language when you were a baby, you also learned the specific dialect of that language that you speak every day. You learned to walk and run, laugh and cry, smile and frown, and any number of other actions, simply because you had not yet convinced yourself that you couldn't. Does saying it that way give you a little different perspective on what the Savior meant when he commanded us to "become as little children, [or] ye shall not enter into the kingdom of heaven" (Matthew 18:3)?

Then my final comments about what is possible for us all come from the brilliant mind of Arthur C. Clarke, the gifted science fiction writer and observer of the human condition. These are knows as Clarke's Three Laws.

Law #1: "When a distinguished but elderly scientist states that something is possible, he is almost certainly right. When he states that something is impossible, he is very probably wrong."

Law #2: "The only way of discovering the limits of the possible is to venture a little way past them into the impossible."

Law #3: "Any sufficiently advanced technology is indistinguishable from magic."

So stretch your mind a bit, become as a little child, and try to find one or two more productive methods of dealing with the challenges that come your way.

Back to Linda's analogy

In my earlier comments about Linda's analogy about our child, I mentioned how respectful it is of the individual needs of each person. What follows is an explanation of the importance of a few of the statements, an examination of the words involved, and a few ways that different people might interpret them.

The choices you have made are not your heart or your spirit.

While the entire analogy has this idea at its core, it is wonderfully appropriate to state it so directly and to do it so early in what she has written.

Put away the shame you feel . . . Recognize how precious you are.

Once again, thoughts that are key to the whole analogy and the purpose for which it was written.

The choices you have made are like clothes.

Using this analogy makes behavior into something that is easier to change because it is such a complete shift from a more traditional or entrenched perspective. By reframing behavior or attitudes into something as changeable as clothing, our mind is much more prepared to consider different choices and approaches than it would be otherwise. After all, we change clothes on a daily basis, and a large percentage of us are always interested in a different or more appealing look.

The rest of the paragraph is used to reinforce the basic comparison between clothing and behavior, which further prepares the reader for a new approach and perspective on their life.

You didn't realize that it didn't really fit you . . . You didn't realize you had anything else to wear.

After everything you have read to this point, I hope you recognize these statements as a redirection of focus from old ideas and attitudes towards the availability of new and different ones. In addition, the statements are made very personal by the use of the "you" perspective, which also gives implicit permission for the reader to take the statement to any conclusion that they might choose, while at the same time gently closing the door on past behavior by stating that the old clothes did not fit.

Clothes that express your own style and personality.

This is another wonderful example of giving permission for a new approach, and even more important, basing that new approach on individual needs rather than meeting the expectations of others.

That outfit doesn't fit you at all now. You close the drawer and walk away, wearing your beautiful new clothes.

Talk about closing the door and moving on. While these statements are phrased in a gentler and less intimidating way than they might have been, they are still very definitive in their intent. The hearer is being told that it is time to move on to the new ideas that are available and that going back would be less comfortable than it was before. They are also told that the new ideas are more appropriate and comfortable than the old ones.

When you are ready . . .

I can't imagine a better way of showing complete respect for the feelings of the individual reader. Everything must be done in the time frame that makes the most sense to each of us as individuals. The only thing that might be added to speed the process would be an open-ended but defined time frame, such as "in a week or two" or "in the next few weeks."

Throw it away.

What better way to leave something behind permanently than throwing it away? Permission has been given, but once again, the timing is at the discretion of the individual.

You will not even remember that you wore it.

Complete personal forgiveness is the most important outcome of all. Why is this so? Because most of us are far less willing to forgive ourselves than Father is. He stands ready and willing to forgive and forget if we will simply change our lives by conforming to his laws. But we like to hold on to the old hurts because a good percentage of the time it is less intimidating than trying something new.

Wear your new clothes proudly.

Could there be a better way to close the analogy than by giving permission for the reader to enjoy their new life and new perspectives? The difference between being proud—the sin of elevating self above others—and a simple acknowledgment of personal accomplishment or improvement, makes all the difference for our lives. This simple closing statement makes it okay for the reader to enjoy their newfound success and gives great hope for further progress and improvement.

Back to the greatest perspective shift of them all

And so we are back to where we started, because we are back to the point of discussing the real message of the gospel of Jesus Christ. Each of us—yes, especially you—has access to the miracles of physical, emotional, and spiritual healing made available only in and through the Atonement of our precious Savior. This can only mean that when we have a proper understanding of the gospel and our place in it, we truly do live in a "no-limits" world, which once again means that the *only* limitations in our world are the ones that we place on ourselves. For the Savior teaches us,

> What greater witness can you have than from God?
>
> Fear not to do good, my sons, for whatsoever ye sow, that shall ye also reap; therefore, if ye sow good ye shall also reap good for your reward.
>
> Therefore, fear not, little flock; do good; let earth and hell combine against you, for if ye are built upon my rock, they cannot prevail.
>
> Behold, I do not condemn you; go your ways and sin no more; perform with soberness the work which I have commanded you.
>
> Look unto me in every thought; doubt not, fear not.
>
> Behold the wounds which pierced my side, and also the prints of the nails in my hands and feet; be faithful, keep my commandments, and ye shall inherit the kingdom of heaven. Amen. (D&C 6:23, 33–37)

Now then, does it not seem more than a little inconsistent to say that you believe in the revealed doctrines of the kingdom of heaven—including all of the glorious truths revealed to Joseph Smith and those who have followed him—and then try to convince yourself that's just the way you are and there is nothing you can do about it? When you compare that approach to the true doctrine that states you can become as Father is, do you begin to recognize the perspective shift that is needed in your thinking?

I know it isn't easy, but I also know it is possible. I promise you that if you will carefully ponder the things you have read under this principle heading, you can come to the same understanding, and that doing so will be one of the most rewarding and inspiring experiences that you will have in all of eternity.

Final comments on this principle

The chapters under this principle heading are intended to give a *very* brief overview of how we think and learn. But remember back at the beginning of the chapter when I said I wanted to motivate you to do some reading? If you are now motivated in that direction, please refer to the following sources and concepts for complete information on the three principal motivational and therapeutic approaches described throughout this chapter.

1. *Psycho-Cybernetics*, by Dr. Maxwell Maltz. Even though it is over forty years old now, there are few books that provide a more detailed and simple blueprint for the process of reprogramming your own brain. This would be undergraduate-level learning.

2. Neuro-Linguist Programming (NLP). This approach to defining how our brains function has been around since the late seventies and has become widely accepted and used in the mental health industry. Any Internet search engine will provide a large number of sources about the specifics of NLP. This would be graduate-level learning.

3. NLP came about largely because of its developer's interest in the groundbreaking work of the late Dr. Milton H. Erickson, a psychiatrist who used the power of suggestion and hypnosis and wrote very extensively about the subject.

Dr. Erickson was born in 1902 and died in 1980. His life was a great example of our ability to deal positively with a series of different challenges. He was born color blind and contracted polio at the age of nineteen. Polio was probably the greatest blessing of his life because he became determined to cure himself of the effects of polio by teaching himself to walk again. He began the process by modeling the movements of small babies in his family as they began learning to move their hands and legs. By following these examples, Dr. Erickson was able to relearn how to walk, but of far greater importance were the sensory perceptions that he developed and his expanded awareness of non-verbal communication, which became extremely acute.

There is an almost total lack of information available to the general public about hypnosis, and the use of hypnosis as a mental health treatment process in particular. I hope that after everything you have read thus far it is plainly obvious that I would never even consider discussing, let alone using, anything that would actually take away my own agency. Nothing is of greater value to me than my agency, and I assure you that while it is possible to use hypnosis to help in the process of shifting perspectives and attitudes, making a subject into some kind of robot or computer program *is not* part of the process.

Pursuing additional information about Dr. Erickson and his amazing life and career is doctorate-level work and not to be undertaken lightly. His writings and seminars are a treasure trove of information, insight, and understanding of the human brain and its most subtle workings. I highly recommend his insight and approaches, but they are not for the easily discouraged.

Principle Four

Tuning the Receiver—Little Things Make a Big Difference

4.1 All Things Are Spiritual

ONE OF THE MOST IMPORTANT TRUTHS THAT WE CAN ever learn is revealed in section 29 of the Doctrine and Covenants, verse 34, which reads, "Wherefore, verily I say unto you that *all* things unto me are spiritual, and not at *any* time have I given unto you a law which was temporal; neither any man, nor the children of men; neither Adam, your father, whom I created" (italics added).

My favorite description of our condition here in mortality is found in a saying that is common among Christians of many denominations: "We are not mortal beings having a spiritual experience; we are spiritual beings having a mortal experience."

And once again, there is this little gem of a scripture: "For as he thinketh in his heart, so is he" (Proverbs 23:7).

So, according to Father, everything in life is spiritual—and as we learned under the last principle heading, our opinions, beliefs, and actions all come about because of our thoughts.

My reason for starting with these concepts is the perspective that they give to our lives, in that they define the nature of our existence here in mortality very precisely. If *everything* we think, do, feel, or say, does in fact have a spiritual component to it, if *every* experience we *ever* have has the things of the Spirit as its first and most important component, if the great God of the universe takes the time to tell us in a rather pointed manner that *absolutely everything* is spiritual to him; then I believe that nothing can ever be more important than increasing our understanding of how our thoughts, attitudes, and actions affect the Spirit of the Lord and its ability to influence our lives.

And so we come to what I believe is the real heart of the matter, for it is my firm conviction that next to an understanding of the Fall of Adam and the Atonement of Jesus Christ, there is nothing more important for us to gain an understanding of than the impact that an increase or decrease in our ability to both recognize and feel the Spirit has on *all* areas of our lives.

Section 19 of the Doctrine and Covenants contains some of the most moving and personal words that the Savior has ever given us about the experiences that were involved in the Atonement, but I believe that there is far more going on than just a recitation of his personal reaction to those experiences. I believe that as important as it is for us to understand the magnitude of his suffering, of far greater significance is what he tells us that we need to learn from the specifics of his experiences.

There is no place in all of scripture that better defines the impact of the loss of the Spirit than what follows, so please pay very close attention.

> Therefore I command you to repent—repent, lest I smite you by the rod of my mouth, and by my wrath, and by my anger, and your sufferings be sore—how sore you know not, how exquisite you know not, yea, how hard to bear you know not.
>
> For behold, I, God, have suffered these things for all, that they might not suffer if they would repent;
>
> But if they would not repent they must suffer even as I;
>
> Which suffering caused myself, even God, the greatest of all, to tremble because of pain, and to bleed at every pore, and to suffer both body and spirit—and would that I might not drink the bitter cup, and shrink—
>
> Nevertheless, glory be to the Father, and I partook and finished my preparations unto the children of men.
>
> Wherefore, I command you again to repent, lest I humble you with my almighty power; and that you confess your sins, lest you suffer these punishments of which I have spoken, *of which in the smallest, yea even in the least degree you have tasted at the time I withdrew my Spirit.* (D&C 19:15–20; italics added)

It has been my experience that when these verses are read and discussed we more often than not stop reading before the last verse, as though what is being taught is only about the Savior's suffering in the garden and on the cross. But I believe that as critical as it is for us to understand his experiences there—after all, what could possibly be more important that expanding our understanding of the Atonement?—in this case what follows in verse 20 is the real reason the Lord gets so personal with us in the first place. I know that you just read it, but please read it again, and this time pay special attention to what is said about the withdrawal of the Spirit.

"Wherefore, I command you again to repent, lest I humble you with my almighty power; and that you confess your sins, lest you suffer these punishments of which I have spoken, of which in the smallest, yea even in the least degree you have tasted at the time *I withdrew my Spirit*" (italics added).

When you have read these six verses in the past, have you noticed how many times the word *repent* is used? Have you noticed the phrase, "But if they would not repent they must suffer even as I"? Have you noticed how our precious Savior details an exact parallel between his suffering and that which awaits us if we fail to take advantage of his gift to us?

And prior to right now, have you ever been aware of the fact that when a sin or thoughtless action on your part has caused the withdrawal of the Spirit you are then experiencing "the least degree" of what it feels like to pay the price attached to your own sins?

What follows in the rest of this chapter is my attempt to define the impact that the loss of the Spirit has on our lives. We will make this definition by examining the effects of specific behaviors and the spiritual consequences that are attached to them. As in the previous chapters, parts of what follows will be controversial for some and uncomfortable for others, but it can be no other way. Also, because of the nature of the things we will be discussing, it will be hard to find places to lighten the mood as much as we have in previous chapters. I'll do the best I can, but I hope you will understand the need for the more serious tone.

Little changes make a very big difference—physically.

Early twenty-first century technology provides an interesting analogy about the impact of small changes in our lives. All this analogy requires is an awareness of the basics of installing a satellite TV receiver, something that a glance around your neighborhood should reveal a large percentage of us are familiar with.

Do you remember how big the satellite dishes were twenty years ago? Do you remember how complicated installing and maintaining them was? How amazing a time do we live in that we have access to such a wide variety of television programming through the installation of such a small satellite receiver on the roof? In most cases, the installation and wiring can be done in a few hours, and homeowners install a large percentage of new dishes without needing professional assistance.

The most complicated part of the process is tuning the receiver.

All tuning means is aligning the dish as closely as possible with the satellite, meaning that the dish must be pointed directly at the satellite in geosynchronous orbit some twenty-two thousand miles out in space.

Think about that for just a minute. Think about the process of raising or lowering the dish by two or three degrees, turning it to the left or right by those same small fractions of an inch, and then think about the clarity of the reception on the TV in your family room. If you have installed your own dish you know exactly what I'm talking about, and if you haven't you'll just have to take my word for it. We are talking about adjustments of a quarter of an inch making a major difference in the reception on your TV screen, and if you go above half-inch adjustments you can pretty well kiss you reception good-bye.

So, now that you have the dish on the roof—and you have it properly tuned in—just think of all the programming choices you have. In the current marketplace, it is also possible to watch different programs on different TVs as long as you have multiple receivers in the house. Then take a minute to consider all of the dishes on all of the homes in your neighborhood, and then think of all of the different programming that is fed down from the satellite to receivers all over your area: so many different receivers tuned into the same source, but all of them watching a different program, based on the channel selected at each individual TV set.

And people wonder how it is possible for Father to communicate with so many of us at the same time.

Here is another example of very small adjustments making a huge difference, but you will need to get back on a bike to really understand this one.

Of all the things I have learned over the last fifteen years from riding a bike, the one that I am the most grateful for is the awareness that I now have of the extremely precise design of our bodies. Consider the fact that when I clip in for a ride, my body is going to be in the same basic position for from one and a half to six hours, or even more on long rides. At a typical cadence of ninety RPM, which equals 5,400 turns of the cranks in any given hour, if you extend that out over a five and a half–hour one hundred–mile ride, it's just under thirty thousand revolutions.

So, finding a position on the bike that allows the most power to be generated, while still being physically comfortable, is the single most important part of any riding experience.

Positioning, you ask? What in the world do you mean by positioning? You buy a bike, bring it home, get on, and ride, right?

Well, if all you are doing is riding around the block that would be fine. But as soon as you hit the open road and are going to be on the bike for more than a few minutes, if your body is out of its optimal position by more than a couple of millimeters you will begin to experience some very unpleasant sensations. By unpleasant I mean things like pain and numbness in your hands from too much pressure being applied to two different nerve groups; pain between your shoulders that can get severe enough to cause cramps between your shoulder blades; anything from stress and pressure to full-on cramps in any and all of the major muscle groups from your lower back to your feet; hot spots on the bottoms of your feet that make them feel like they are on fire; and there are other things that can happen that are even more unpleasant than those just listed.

Like I said, sanity is not a requirement to be a cyclist.

So, how do you eliminate all of the fun and games described above? You get your body into *exactly* the right position on the bike. How do you do that? You raise or lower you saddle until it is at the *exact* height for your body and your riding style. Then you move the saddle fore or aft until it is in *exactly* the right position for your body and your riding style. And finally, you may need to buy a new stem for the handlebars to move your hands either closer to or farther away from your body.

Right about now you're probably thinking something along the lines of *That doesn't sound too difficult*, but I assure you that finding your "perfect" position can take more than one or two adjustments and can have some very interesting side effects along the way.

So, how do you find that perfect position? You start with a few general guidelines and then figure it out as you go. How do you figure it out? Your body will tell you in unmistakable terms when it likes the position you are in and when it doesn't. How does it tell you? Just go back and read the list above. If any of those things are present, something is off in your positioning.

Simply put, your position on the bike is the single most important mechanical consideration in your ability to pedal hard for any period of time at all.

Now then, when I mentioned a rider's position being off by a couple of millimeters just a bit ago I hope you didn't think I was being dramatic, because that really is the amount of adjustment we are talking about here. Moving your saddle height more than two or three millimeters between rides feels like a difference of an inch or two, and moving it by two millimeters during a ride feels like a foot. Your positioning may only be off by one or two millimeters, but that is enough to make the difference between an enjoyable ride and a day of pure misery.

Even though I have been doing it for fifteen years now, I am constantly amazed at the incredible precision of my body and its ability to communicate exactly how it feels and what it needs to keep going. And we haven't even mentioned nutrition yet, but that subject will come up a little farther down the road, so let's keep rolling.

Little changes make a big difference—spiritually.

We currently live in the physical world, and Newton's Third Law of Motion about that physical world states, "For every action there is an equal and opposite reaction." From there, because God says, "*All things* unto me are spiritual" (D&C 29:34; italics added), it would then seem correct to say that every physical action must also have a spiritual reaction, and that the spiritual reaction must be equal to the physical action. The only difference in the analogy between the laws of physics and the laws of the spirit would be the critical distinction that the spiritual reaction is either positive or negative in direct correlation with the nature of the physical action or thought, and not in opposition to it.

So, if we were going to state the spiritual law that would be the equivalent of Newton's third law, it would read something like this: For every physical action or thought, there is an equal and corresponding spiritual reaction.

But how do you quantify what that spiritual reaction is? Since it is almost impossible to answer that question with words, I'm going to fall back on the old adage that a picture is worth at least a thousand of them. But before doing so, there is one other thought that you need to have in place.

It is my experience that it does not matter what specific behavior is being discussed, the spiritual reaction is the same in all cases. That reaction is that as we move closer to or further away from the influence of the Spirit of the Lord, our self-confidence and self-esteem increase or decrease *in direct proportion* to that spiritual movement. As a result, our ability to trust our own thinking and decision-making must also either increase or decrease, once again, *in direct proportion* to that spiritual movement.

With that said, the pictures and captions that follow are the result of an art therapy exercise at the facility where one of our children is currently in treatment. All of the young people were asked to draw their "rock bottom" experience, and these pencil drawings are some of the results of that assignment. As you look at these pictures and read the captions that go with them you should remember that all of these kids are under eighteen years of age.

You will probably be surprised to see how well they draw their own feelings, but more likely you will be shocked at how well they have drawn yours, or at least something close to them. If you do notice some similarities, all that should do is confirm in your mind the accuracy of the statements made above.

I drew myself with a dark hood over my head, representing my state of depression a year ago. The dark eyes represent my blindness, and my mouth is covered and shut off from the world. The smoke represents my drug problem.

My rock bottom was when I was high on meth. I had been awake all night and I got up to look in the mirror. I remember seeing myself, but not seeing what I really was. I saw myself, but I couldn't see how I felt. I was drained physically and emotionally. I was alone. I didn't know where to go.

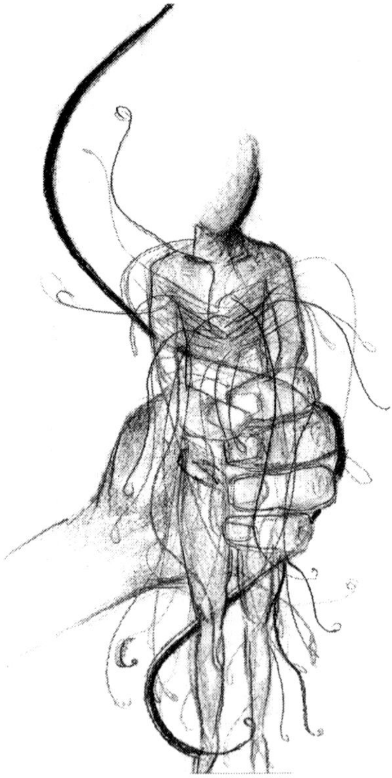

The reason I drew this I guess is because I . . . saw it in my head. At one point in time it was how I felt. It's a person in need being held or squeezed by a fist.

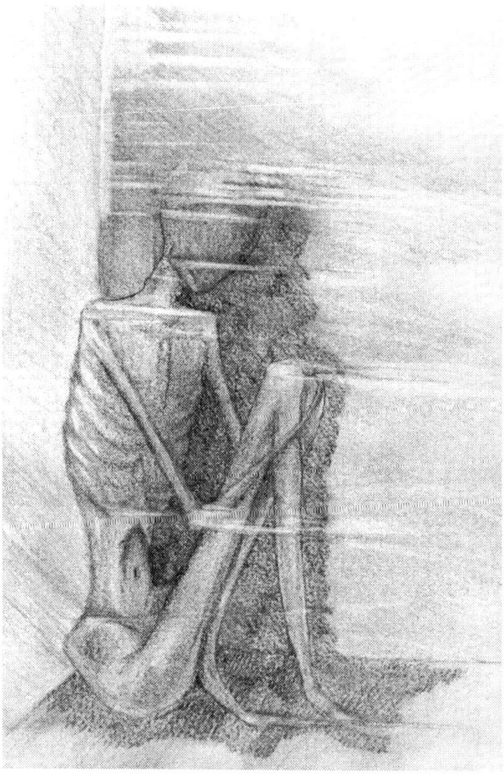

This is my lowest moment, my rock bottom feeling. I hated everything. I hated myself, my life, who and what I had come to stand for. I was no longer a person. I felt more like a shadow of someone who once was, and what little of me that was left was blown away by the life I had made for myself. I was, in every sense of the word, dead. I was faceless, nameless, just another screw-up kid with no hope or dream for the future.

No matter how often I look at those pictures, it's a shock to my spirit every time I go back to them, so I hope it isn't too much of a shock for you to see them for the first time. However, I find that as I read the captions and ponder on them while looking at the pictures, there is a great clarity that comes to my thinking on this subject. How so? Because they are so devastatingly accurate in their depiction and descriptions of the many different affects that the loss of the Spirit has on our lives.

So, once again, as spiritual beings having a mortal experience, there cannot be anything that is more critical for us to learn to recognize than the impact that gaining or losing the Spirit has on our lives. And because we have already established the fact that our thoughts *always* precede our actions, it should then be even more obvious why we must always be striving to increase our understanding of how our thinking leads to our actions, and the effect that those actions have on the corresponding availability of the Spirit.

4.2 Common Thinking Errors
Definitions and Examples

FOR THE NEXT THREE CHAPTERS WE WILL EXAMINE some of the more prevalent and damaging thinking and behavioral errors of our time. We will start with some basic thinking errors by listing a short statement about each thought process, followed by a few comments. It should be noted that some of these statements come directly from the rehab environment, while others are based on more traditional treatment approaches. Once we have finished with the thinking errors, we will move to some of the more common behavioral errors that are part of our world, and we will finish with what I hope is a healing and helpful perspective on all of these different challenges. So, let's begin.

"Your best thinking got you here."

Another way of saying this would be, "Your best choices got you to this point in your life." Depending on the circumstances of your life right now, those statements can either give you great reinforcement or great cause for concern. How do you feel about your life right now? Are you happy with where you are, or is there lots of room for improvement? And yes, I realize that there is always room for improvement, but are we talking small ones or big ones? And if they are big ones, what does that say about your best thinking?

I'm sorry if that is a little pointed for you, but if you have made it this far you should be ready for that kind of question by now.

This statement is frequently used in the rehab and treatment world, but I think it applies wonderfully to all areas of our lives, and if hearing it put that bluntly helps you realize that your thinking needs some work, so much the better.

"The only way over it is through it" and "if you don't talk it out, you'll act it out."

Another way to think of this is realizing that these are not thinking errors in and of themselves, but they are statements about some of the most common thinking errors in our society.

One of the most dangerous thinking errors we ever make is buying into the idea that we can simply forget about a mistake or problem and just move on, without actually dealing with the issue. Nothing could be further from the truth, and there are few thought patterns that cause more pain and frustration in all three areas of our lives—physical, mental/emotional, and spiritual. In addition, this approach is especially dangerous when we are not the party with the issue, but when someone we love and care about has a problem.

As an example, I recently heard of a situation where one half of a couple had been involved in some serious transgressions before meeting their spouse. After the wedding the one said to the other that it was now inappropriate to even talk about those things because they were in the past and didn't need to be brought up ever again.

That response is one of the coldest, most calloused and selfish things that can ever be said to someone who still needs to deal with a serious behavioral problem or error in thinking. Why is that so? Because it completely invalidates their feelings and emotions about whatever the issue is, and in so doing tramples all over what is usually a bruised and tender spirit. So, as a loving and caring parent, spouse, or friend, we will never have a greater obligation than to be available when needed as a support and sounding board for those who need our love and help. This can only mean that there is no more Christlike service that we can ever give than to help those who are in such desperate need. Just think of how much time your bishop spends doing exactly that, and maybe it will add a little more perspective to the comment.

So suck it up, and just be willing to listen to someone as they talk through their issues and problems. After all, who knows, you may need them to return the favor someday.

"Denial is not a river in Egypt."

Brigham Young said, "Men will continue in self-justification to the damnation of their own souls." Denial is simply an attempt—almost always based on vanity and pride—to minimize the effects of our own negative behavior. Because who among us likes to face our shortcomings head on?

After reading Principle Three's chapters, do you now recognize these thought patterns as being based on "that's just the way I am" thinking? So maybe we should add that one to the mix again too. This would be a good time to go back and review those chapters if you need to refresh your memory.

Consider the fact that nothing ever gives more pleasure to our adversary than when we do not hold ourselves accountable for thoughts and actions that we know to be wrong. Again, why is this so? Because there are very few things that we can ever do that have a more insidious and damaging effect on our ability to feel and recognize the Spirit. And if you don't understand that comment, maybe you should try reading the Sermon on the Mount again.

"If you always do what you always did, you'll always get what you always got."

Leave it to Albert Einstein, for could there ever be a better definition of insanity than continuing to do what you have always done while expecting a different result? At the subconscious level, that is one of the reasons you keep doing the same old thing—because you know what the outcome will be, and you know how to deal with that outcome, regardless of how unpleasant it may be.

In the Principle Three chapters we said that predictability is one of the most powerful motivators of our behavior. That's because we are creatures of two primary motivators, safety and habit (or pursuing pleasure and avoiding pain if you prefer it said that way). This can only mean that knowing the outcome of any given situation is virtually always preferable to something that is uncertain, once again, even if that outcome is unpleasant.

So, as I have said for a very long time now, "Better the hell I know than the heaven that I don't," which just means that we continue down the same old path simply because the ruts in the trail are so deep that moving our wagon horizontally requires more effort than we are willing to put forth.

"You are where you want to be or you wouldn't be there."

Once again, this is not a thinking error by itself, but it is a great statement about how our thinking gets us to where we are. If you want to change where you are, you have to change your thinking about where you want to be, and hence the need for all of the information contained in Principle Three on the basics of how you make such changes. So get started already!

"If only I . . ." or "If only you . . ." thinking

You know this one—If only I were thinner, if only I were prettier, if only you made more money, if only you were nicer to me, if only . . . if only . . . if only. We could go on for hours about this one, but are you to the point that you recognize this one as an attempt to blame your problems on a person or circumstance that you would like to believe is beyond your control? Or are you starting to get a bit more comfortable with the reality that you are the person with all the power in your own life and that it's time for you to step up and take charge of where you're going and what you're doing? If so, I am thrilled for you, and if not, hang in there and keep reading; we're not done yet.

"All or nothing" or perfectionistic thinking

These are two of the most dangerous thinking errors of all. As a result, these kinds of thinking are involved in a large percentage of family violence and violence-toward-self situations. Examples of "all or nothing" thinking would be, "If I can't have you then no one can" or "It's my way or the highway." Perfectionistic thinking might include "Why try? I always screw things up anyway" or "I'm such a screw up that the world would be better off without me in it."

But here is an interesting comparison to these kinds of thinking: "Giving line upon line, precept upon precept; here a little, and there a little; giving us consolation by holding forth that which is to come, confirming our hope!" (D&C 128:21; see also Isaiah 28:10).

So at least Father understands that we are not able to do everything perfectly all the time, even if we don't always understand it ourselves. But the far more important question is, Are you beginning to recognize how holding yourself to an impossible standard can cause some very significant spiritual problems, along with the emotional and psychological ones we have already mentioned?

And here are three tough ones for you:

"Don't talk. Don't trust. Don't feel—especially if you're male."

You have heard all of the little sayings about these three issues: "Tough guys don't cry," "Real men don't have feelings," "Talking is for sissies," "You can't trust anyone," and on and on.

Yet we are constantly confronted with the emotional devastation caused by the rampant abuse of the young, we are repeatedly reminded of the psychological damage done in wartime and other life-threatening situations, and we are barraged with information about the after-effects of psychological and physical abuse of both men and women. So can we please get past the false bravado that is required to maintain such a façade? Why is this so important? Because such an approach takes far more energy and focus to maintain than any real protection that can possibly be provided.

Can we also admit that giving our full and complete trust to anyone is a major problem for all of us? After all, none of us got through childhood without at least a few traumatic experiences, and it's obvious that some have far more than most. But none of that means that we have to allow those experiences to continue dominating our lives and thinking once we are adults. For once again, isn't the entire plan of salvation based on the opportunity that it affords us to learn from our experiences and improve our lives with that learning? And can we please get to the point that we are willing to talk about our feelings and emotional needs so that those closest to us can stop guessing about what we need and how to treat us?

Why is it so critically important for us to do things in this new way? Because until we do so, all of the fear, pain, guilt, frustration, and anger that are part and parcel with these approaches festers until there is some kind of an explosion, either that or a complete emotional shutdown. Because until we learn to deal with and control our emotions, they will dominate our lives and control our thoughts and actions, thereby condemning us to the kind of living hell that only the adversary could enjoy or approve of.

Because until we do so, we are not only shutting out those who know us well enough—and love us enough—to actually help in the process, but we are also shutting ourselves off from the one thing that can provide the peace and healing that we so desperately need: the Holy Spirit of God.

As a further example of the importance of having that Spirit involved in the healing process, please consider the following: "For whoso is faithful unto the obtaining these two priesthoods of which I have spoken, and the magnifying their calling, are sanctified by the Spirit *unto the renewing of their bodies*" (D&C 84:33, italics added).

If you want the best examples that there are of the reality of this statement, just observe President Hinckley and several of the other Apostles, who, though well advanced in years, are able to maintain schedules that would be physically and emotionally debilitating for the majority of men half their age.

Here are a few more statements of truth:

- *Someone has to go forward so that others know there is somewhere to go forward to.* It's always easier to find our way when there is a guide to help show us the way, but when we are talking about finding new behaviors or thought processes, this concept is even more important. And if we were expected to figure everything out for ourselves, why would Father need to call apostles and prophets or provide us with parents to guide and teach us?
- *Secrets have power.* Unfortunately that power is usually negative, because something that needs to stay a secret is also virtually always negative. After all, none of us like to admit our shortcomings or faults, and we really hate to own our mistakes. As it is so eloquently put by the title of a wonderful little book, *Feelings Buried Alive Never Die.*
- *A lie unchallenged becomes the truth.* One of the most unfortunate traits of all humanity is, "A lie told often enough becomes the truth" (Kahlil Gibran). And in the words of Sir Winston Churchill, "Men occasionally stumble over the truth, but most of them pick themselves up and hurry off as though nothing ever happened." It's also far easier to examine the thinking of others than it is our own, and so we live with lots of lies in our lives simply because we aren't willing to challenge our own thinking very often.

- *Pain is inevitable—suffering is optional.* As explained previously, it is impossible to overstate the importance of our attitude in dealing with the challenges and trials of life. Remember, "One persons hangnail is another's severed limb." But if you choose to suffer emotionally because of the actions of another, just make sure that you do it in a huge way so that it can be all the more enjoyable for you. After all, there must be a positive payoff for you somewhere in all of that or you wouldn't keep doing it.
- *Hurt people hurt people.* Could there ever be a better example of this one than to remind ourselves that the adversary wants us all to be "miserable like unto himself" (2 Nephi 2:27)? Kind of the ultimate "hurt" person, don't you think? But in today's world there are libraries that could be filled with the books that detail the damage done to and by those who have been abused in some fashion or another, and who have then acted out even more horrible abuses onto others in a vain attempt to deal with the pain caused by their abuser.
- *You can never have enough of what you don't need.* An old saying from AA says, "One drink is too many, and a million aren't enough." A bigger house, a faster car, a new bicycle, a new wife or husband, a new nose, and the list goes on and on. Where or when does it stop? Only when we come to understand that none of those "things" is enough, and that real happiness can only come from who and what we are and not from what we have.
- *Facts can't be changed; opinions can.* Try as we might, we can't change the laws of physics, or much of anything else for that matter. But what is possible is to learn as much as we can about real truth, and then either conform our opinions and behavior to those facts or continue paying the price for our unwillingness to learn from our mistakes.

4.3 Common Behavioral Errors

What You Do Physically Matters Spiritually

IN THIS PORTION OF OUR JOURNEY WE WILL BE discussing a combination of physical actions, additional thinking errors, and the combined effects that come from these most destructive choices. We will once again list an error or group of errors and then comment on them.

Physical addictions, specifically drugs and alcohol

Given the predominance of these problems in our home, it should not come as a surprise that I start with this one.

There are very few things in the modern world that are better documented than the physical and psychological destruction caused by the abuse of narcotics and other addictive agents in all their varieties. It should also come as no surprise that the principle reason for these substances being so readily available is the incentive for monetary gain.

Those who have not tried any kind of drugs cannot comprehend the attraction, and those who have cannot explain it, but what follows is a better explanation of the effects than I could ever come up with. The author of this poem is unknown. It's not pretty, but it is very important.

> "My name is Crystal Meth"
>
> I destroy homes, I tear families apart,
> I take your children away from you, and that's just the start.
>
> I am more costly than diamonds, more precious than gold.
> The sorrow I bring is a sight to behold.

If you need me, I'm easily found;
I live all around you—in schools and most towns.

I live with the rich. I live with the poor.
I live down the street and maybe next door.

I'm made in a lab but not like you think:
I can be made under the kitchen sink,
In your child's closet, and even the woods.
If this scares you to death, it certainly should.

I have many names, but there's one you know best.
I'm sure you've heard of me; my name is Crystal Meth.

My power is awesome—try me, you'll see.
But if you do, you may never break free.

Just try me once and I might let you go,
But try me twice and I'll own your soul.

When I possess you, you'll steal and you'll lie.
You'll do what you have to—just to get high.

The crimes you'll commit for my narcotic charms
Will be well worth the pleasure you'll feel in your
Lungs, nose, and arms.

You'll lie to your mother and steal from your dad.
When you see their tears, you should feel sad.

You'll forget your morals and how you were raised.
I'll be your conscience, and I'll teach you my ways.

I take parents from kids and kids from their parents;
I turn people away from God, and separate friends.

I'll take everything from you, your looks and your pride.
I'll be with you always—right by your side.

You'll give up everything—your family and your home,
Your friends and your money, and then you'll be alone.

I'll take and take, till you have nothing more to give.
When I'm finished with you, you'll be lucky to live.

If you try me, be warned—this is no game.
If you give me a chance, I'll drive you insane.

I'll ravish your body; I'll control your mind;
I'll own you completely; your soul will be mine.

The nightmares I'll give you while you're lying in bed.
The voices you'll hear will be from inside your head.
The sweats, the shakes, the visions you'll see.
I want you to know, these are all gifts from me.

By then it's too late and you'll know in your heart,
That you are mine and we shall never part.

You'll regret that you tried me—they always do—
But you came to me, not I to you.

You knew this would happen, many times you were told,
But you challenged my power and chose to be bold.

You could have said no and just walked away.
If you could live that day over, now, what would you say?

I'll be your master; you'll be my slave.
I'll even go with, when you go to your grave.

Now that you've met me, what will you do?
Will you try me or not? It's all up to you.

I can bring you more misery than words can tell.
Come take my hand; let me lead you to hell!

Now it is time to go, by which means you know.
I'm following my master with another line of blow.

I would suggest that the effects of drug use and addictive agents of any kind are so similar that you could substitute any one of them in place of crystal meth in the above title without needing to change it much at all. But then, such is the plan of the adversary, for he does not care at all what the method of enslavement is, so long as our ability to exercise our agency is compromised or destroyed, and we are thus bound and lead carefully down to hell.

Unmarried sexual involvement in all its different forms

There are few things that cause more grief and pain—and even fewer that cause more debate, confusion, frustration, and anger—than those included under this heading. The heading has been made intentionally broad, so that it includes all forms of sexual involvement, because that is in fact the most appropriate way to discuss the subject.

Why, you ask? Because, once again, it does not matter in the least what form of sexual sin you want to talk about, the end result is the same for all of them. It must also be acknowledged that though some subjects under this heading are more frequently and hotly debated than others, that does not change the fact that sexual sin in any form is still sin, and the specifics involved are of far smaller significance than are the common consequences.

Also, while every other subject dealt with in this book is based primarily on my own understanding, observations, and experiences, this one cannot be adequately addressed without relying heavily on a specific general conference talk. Elder Jeffrey R. Holland gave a talk entitled "Personal Purity" on Sunday, October 4, 1998, and it contains, in my estimation, the most comprehensive comments yet given on the subject. I obviously cannot include the entire text here, but I strongly urge you to read and reread it in its entirety for a more complete understanding of what follows here.

Early in the talk Elder Holland quotes the following: "Can a man take fire in his bosom, and his clothes not be burned? Can one go upon hot coals, and his feet not be burned? . . . Whoso committeth adultery . . . destroyeth his own soul. A wound and dishonour shall he get; and his reproach shall not be wiped away" (Proverbs 6:27–28, 32–33).

He then continues to detail three specific reasons unmarried sexual relations in any form is so serious:

> First is the revealed, restored doctrine of the human soul. . . . The body is an essential part of the soul. This distinctive and very important Latter-day Saint doctrine underscores why sexual sin is so serious. We declare that one who uses the God-given body of another without divine sanction abuses the very soul of that individual. . . . In exploiting the body of another—which means exploiting his or her soul—one desecrates the Atonement of Christ, which saved that soul and which makes possible the gift of eternal life. And when one mocks the Son of Righteousness, one steps into a realm of heat hotter and holier than the noonday sun. You cannot do so and not be burned.

Elder Holland then gives an even more specific and stunning reason as to why this is the case. "Why? Well, for one reason because of the incalculable suffering in both body and spirit endured by the Savior of the world so that we *could* flee. We owe Him something for that. Indeed, we owe Him everything for that. 'Ye are not your own,' Paul says. 'Ye [have been] bought with a price: therefore glorify God in your body, and in your spirit, which are God's.' In sexual transgression the soul is at stake—the body and the spirit."

I remember when these specific words were spoken from the pulpit, and feeling as though the whole world was spinning around me; my head reeled at the magnitude of what had just been said. But Elder Holland was just getting warmed up. Remember, there are three reasons that he was going to give, and so far you have only heard one of them.

> Secondly, may I stress that human intimacy is reserved for a married couple because it is the ultimate symbol of total union, a totality and a union ordained and defined by God. From the Garden of Eden onward, marriage was intended to mean the complete merger of a man and a woman—their hearts, hopes, lives, love, family, future, everything. . . .
>
> But such a total union, such an unyielding commitment between a man and a woman, can only come with the proximity and permanence afforded in a marriage covenant, with solemn promises and the pledge of all they possess—their very hearts and minds, all their days and all their dreams.
>
> Can you see the moral schizophrenia that comes from *pretending* you are one, pretending you have made solemn promises before God, sharing the physical symbols and the physical intimacy of your counterfeit union but then fleeing, retreating, severing all such other aspects of what was meant to be a total obligation? . . .
>
> To give illicitly that which is not yours to give (remember, "you are not your own") and to give only part of that which cannot be followed with the gift of your whole self is emotional Russian roulette. If you persist in pursuing physical satisfaction without the sanction of heaven, you run the terrible risk of such spiritual, psychic damage that you may undermine *both* your longing for physical intimacy *and* your ability to give wholehearted devotion to a later, truer love.

Moral schizophrenia! Emotional Russian roulette! Could there be a better definition of the effects of any form of sexual activity outside the bonds of marriage than those five words? I am convinced that it is impossible to articulate a better one, so please study them carefully, ponder on them, and then realize the enormity of our choices in this realm.

And finally he said,

> Thirdly, may I say that physical intimacy is not only a symbolic union between a husband and a wife—the very uniting of their souls—but it is also symbolic of a shared relationship between them and their Father in Heaven. . . .
>
> These are moments when we quite literally unite our will with God's

> will, our spirit with His spirit, where communion through the veil becomes very real. At such moments we not only acknowledge His divinity but we quite literally take something of that divinity to ourselves.

As I have read this talk over and over again, I have become convinced that with these few words Elder Holland has given us the single greatest key that can be given in regards to the importance of physical intimacy. That key is that the act of physical intimacy—as Elder Holland says it, "the very uniting of their souls"—is the best approximation that we can ever have as mortals of the level of unity that we shared with Father before we were born. I further believe that the instincts and urges associated with the physical act are simply a manifestation of our almost desperate need to feel that same level of spiritual unity while here in mortality.

I wish I had an appropriately funny story or comment to make here to lighten the mood a bit, but I don't. So let's just say that if you need to take a break and ponder on what you have just read, it is certainly understandable. But as you might guess, we still have lots of ground left to cover, so when you are ready we will move on again.

Same-gender attraction

I approach this subject with an overwhelming awareness of my own inadequacy, not because I fear the subject, but because I respect and admire so many who choose to live this lifestyle. I have several good friends who live the homosexual lifestyle. These are good and decent people who are tremendously talented and make many positive and wonderful contributions to our society in general and to my life in particular. As I interact with them I do everything I possibly can to avoid giving offense, and on the whole our interaction is without conflict. Yet the subject must be addressed in a doctrinally sound and morally honest manner.

And so I state without hesitation or reservation, physical relations between those of the same-gender—male with male or female with female—is a sin for exactly the same reason that relations between unmarried men and women is a sin.

And what is that reason? Simply because God, our eternal Father, has decreed it to be so. In another general conference talk, President Boyd K. Packer gave needed clarity to this comment when he said, "We did not make the rules; they were revealed as commandments. We do not cause nor can we prevent the consequences if you disobey the moral laws. . . . In spite of criticism or opposition, we must teach and we must warn."[1]

In our modern world, much is made of the importance and influence of genetics on our thoughts, actions, choices, and lives. It is an everyday occurrence to hear voices from virtually every corner of science and philosophy—and even some from the world of theology—telling us that same-gender attraction is not a choice, that genetics hold sway in all things, and that we are slaves to actions beyond our control. We are further bombarded with societal pressures of heretofore unimaginable proportions that demand acceptance of that which is plainly contrary to the command of Almighty God. And after all of that, those who stand firm in the face of such demands are accused of intolerance and bigotry. We are accused of being narrowminded and shallow simply because we cannot change Father's own eternal standards, and the war of words is escalated to a fever pitch in an attempt to gain even a toehold of emotional approval and acceptance.

But rather than continue the war of words as a scientific or philosophical exercise, let's see if some reasoning, and an unexpected comparison, can shed some additional light on the subject.

The reasoning involved is actually very simple. For if, as was detailed in Principle One, Father is a God of truth and cannot lie, and if as a perfect being it is impossible for him to make a mistake, then it should be plainly obvious from what is said in the scriptures that *any* form of sexual relations outside of marriage—regardless of gender attraction or involvement—carries the strictest prohibition possible.

Simply stated, any sexual involvement outside of marriage is unacceptable before the Lord, once again, regardless of the genders involved.

So, why does this issue cause such huge problems for so many? For the same reason that so many other things cause us problems. Because man's wisdom is foolishness to the Lord, or as it is said in the scriptures, "Their wisdom is foolishness and it profiteth them not. And they shall perish" (2 Nephi 9:28).

In addition—yes, here it comes again—where there is no choice, there can be no accountability. If there is no accountability, the plan of salvation collapses, the purposes of creation are brought to naught, God ceases to be God, chaos reigns, and the adversary and those who follow him revel in their victory.

Which brings us to what I believe—though it would not commonly be recognized as such—is a reasonable comparison of the thinking patterns involved with any of these subjects.

There are very few things more incomprehensible to most of us than the eating disorder known as anorexia, yet there is a significant and ever growing number of people who are affected by this issue. A simple medical definition helps to make the comparison at hand:

> Anorexia: An eating disorder characterized by markedly reduced appetite or total aversion to food. Anorexia is a serious psychological disorder. It is a condition that goes well beyond out-of-control dieting. The person with anorexia . . . initially begins dieting to lose weight. Over time, the weight loss becomes a sign of mastery and control. The drive to become thinner is thought to be secondary to concerns about control and fears relating to one's body. The individual continues the endless cycle of restrictive eating, often to a point close to starvation. This becomes an obsession and is similar to an addiction to a drug.[2]

So, this definition tells us that anorexia is a psychological condition that manifests itself through extreme dieting and weight loss, but that it really deals with concerns about body image and self-control.

Is it just me, or does that sound like thoughts preceding actions to you too?

Then because body/self image and self-control are also at the heart of most of our other behaviors—especially those related to sexuality—can we not then make the connection between our thoughts and our sexual tendencies too? Could there possibly be a better word than *obsession* to describe the preoccupation with all things sexual that dominates today's society, and what do you think of this definition's comparison between these thought processes and actual drug addiction?

And finally, what do you think is really happening when one anorexic looks at another and says, "You are too thin, and you don't look healthy at all," while still being unable to acknowledge her own deterioration and failing health?

But here is the greater point to all of this. (You were hoping there was one in here somewhere, right?) The point to all of this is agency—your absolute right to choose, and this life as a test, providing opportunities for you to learn by your own undeniable experience. And remember, thoughts *always* leading to behavior. Do you now recognize the critical significance of the order in which these subjects have been addressed?

For if we truly understand these ideas first—and especially if we are now willing to acknowledge our behavior as nothing but repeating patterns that are almost entirely based on our own thinking—it should give us the hope of being able to address all of these issues with more productive, personally fulfilling, and spiritually appropriate methods.

Pornography

Even after acknowledging the devastating problems caused by physical addiction in all of its forms, the mental addiction to pornography leads to even greater problems—including ever increasing forms of psychological and spiritual illness—than anything we have talked about thus far. It is true that all of these problems seem to go hand in hand, but in the same sense that marijuana and beer are the gateways to the misery of physical addiction, pornography is the gateway to virtually all of the sexual problems we see in the world today.

As such, it is impossible to overstate the impact of pornography on the physical and spiritual well-being of a large percentage of the world's population. Then, given our previous definition of the impact that everything we see, hear, or think has on our ability to align our spiritual receiver with the Spirit of God, is it not obvious why pornography's impact is even more pronounced on those who would seek to have a personal and healing relationship with God, our Father, through the instrumentality of the Holy Ghost?

And if pornography has that kind of impact on our ability to feel the Spirit, what kind of impact do you think it has on our ability to righteously exercise power in the priesthood?

Thus, it cannot be an overstatement to say that pornography is the single greatest challenge currently faced by the men of the world and the Church, regardless of their age. This is true because of the omnipresence of the Internet and the resulting ease with which absolutely anyone anywhere can access the most graphic, degrading, and spiritually debilitating material ever seen in the whole history of the world.

Further, it should not come as a surprise that the adversary would use every possible method of distortion, lying, confrontation, and trickery at his disposal to attack what Father clearly intends to be one of the most sacred and spiritually healing experiences we can have in all of mortality. It should also then be obvious that the only possible outcome of following after Satan's approach is a level of emotional, physical, and spiritual degradation that can only lead to both serious and long-term problems in all three areas. Not to be redundant, but he is still "the father of all lies," and he wishes all men to be "miserable like unto himself" (2 Nephi 2:18, 27).

This is also the point in the conversation where someone involved with pornography usually asks something like, "What difference does it make? It's only a few harmless pictures or a couple of short videos. What's the big deal?"

In answer, please consider the three things that are at the heart of the problems caused by pornography:

- The objectification of women and the degradation that comes with that second-class status
- The creation of horribly distorted concepts of an appropriate female body image
- The unrealistic and degrading portrayals of female sexuality and desire

All of these happen because we men are such visual creatures, meaning that the pictures we allow into or create within our own minds are almost always the first and most powerful representations of and motivators for our behavior. Then, because those same pictures are associated with such powerful feelings and emotions that create both desire and expectation, because our resulting understanding of sexuality becomes so warped and distorted, *and because the effect on our thinking and spirit is so subtle over time*, our ability to have the unifying, uplifting, and healing experience that Father intended is severely compromised at best, and there are far too many examples of it being completely destroyed.

Imagine going through life feeling that there are only two things you are good for. One of those is to bear and raise children, and the other is to make yourself available for any form of sexual activity that might be desired at the drop of a hat. I can only speak for myself, but that's not much of a life. Yet it is the lot of far too many women the world over, and pornography is the single greatest contributor to that second-class status. Because of the omnipresence of the effects of pornography on the world at large, the glory and honor that were afforded Mother Eve are rarely available to her daughters today, and so the adversary revels in his perceived victory while Father weeps at the emptiness and hopelessness that so many feel.

So, what can be done to deal with the effects of this monster?

First, we must acknowledge the ability of the Holy Ghost to cleanse us of the long-term effects—the absence of the Spirit being chief among them—that are caused by addiction to pornography. This cleansing can only happen because of the Atonement and sacrifice of the Lord Jesus Christ.

Second, we must not only change the things that we look at with our physical eyes, but we must also take *complete* control of the images that we allow ourselves to look at within the confines of our own mind. To do so we must learn even more about the processes and techniques described in the earlier chapters and then use them on a daily basis to literally reprogram our own brains. Thus the further significance of including those things in the first place should become even more apparent.

Finally, we must be willing to acknowledge that there is very little difference between addiction to pornography and any of the other addictions we have already addressed. Yes, the physical addiction to pornography comes without the presence of an externally administered chemical, but there can be no mistaking the addictive nature of the chemicals produced by the resulting thought patterns of our own brain.

There have been a multitude of talks given and articles written about this issue by those with far more insight than I, both inside and outside the Church. If this is an issue for you, I would urgently recommend you to a research and study of those materials. And once again, if you question the reality of the spiritual effects of this issue, just go back a few pages and look at the pictures again. They still explain it far better than I ever could.

Disregard for our physical body

While you might think that this subject has already been addressed under the headings of physical addiction in all its forms and the sexual issues just detailed, there is another group of physical issues that must be addressed. And as with the comments on same gender attraction, this is not a subject I enjoy bringing up in the first place—as we move forward, it will become very obvious why that is the case—yet this subject is just as important, maybe even more so.

The behaviors involved with this subject include what we eat, how well we maintain our bodies, and the spiritual impact of speeding the process of our own physical deterioration. Once again, there is a spiritual foundation that must be laid before anything else is addressed. In this case that spiritual foundation is found in the New Testament, where Paul says, "Know ye not that ye are the temple of God, and that the Spirit of God dwelleth in you? If any man defile the temple of God, him shall God destroy; for the temple of God is holy, which temple ye are" (1 Corinthians 3:16–17).

In comparing our physical bodies to the temple, Paul makes us keenly aware of the tremendous importance that Father places on this tabernacle of clay, and he further explains the penalty for improperly maintaining this temple. I believe that in using this approach Paul was making a literal comparison, that he was in fact saying that our bodies are temples in the same sense that the temple buildings are, and that if we maintain them properly the Spirit of the Lord will be that much more available to us as a result.

And here is an even more specific scripture to define the importance of this point: "The elements are the tabernacle of God; yea, man is the tabernacle of God, even temples; and whatsoever temple is defiled, God shall destroy that temple" (D&C 93:35). It is also critically important to note the "c" cross-reference at the word *temples*, for that reference refers to "Body, Sanctity of."

There is also a corresponding physical analogy to help make the point, and that analogy once again comes from the world of cycling. A few years ago in October—after he had won either his second or third Tour De France title in July (I don't specifically remember if it was the second or third)—Lance Armstrong actually took two weeks off from the bike. He went two full weeks without riding at all.

Big deal, you think. How much impact could so short a break in training possibly have on a world-class athlete? But because of the technology available in today's world, it is actually possible to answer that question with great accuracy. In this case it took Lance two *months* to get back to the level of fitness he was at before a two-week break in his training.

Now, I will grant you that it took that long because of the combination of his extraordinarily high level of fitness to begin with, and the fact that he is a genetic miracle with astonishingly high levels of natural physical capability. But that does not negate the fact that it took two months of hard work to get back to where he was before taking two weeks off. If we apply that same equation to all things physical, even though my level of fitness is far below that of Lance Armstrong, a corresponding decrease in my fitness will require just as much work from the same amount of laying off, and probably even more.

The real point should be pretty obvious, for if taking a two-week break from training had that much impact on a world-class athlete, how much impact do you think your two-year (or is it two-decade?) break would have on your body? And of far greater significance to this discussion, how much impact would it have on your spirit? I know, I know, I'm being blunt again. But if you've made it this far, you should be used to that by now.

So please consider an interesting comparison of the physical effects involved with two common ways that our bodies are regularly abused. It is an accepted fact that tobacco causes a large percentage of the medical problems that many face today, and that its principle effect is to cause congestion in the respiratory system and organs of the body. The congestion caused by tobacco is primarily focused on the lungs, which obviously results in a decrease in overall energy because of the impact on the body's ability to process oxygen and efficiently deliver it throughout the body.

On the other hand, the effect of excessive weight gain is also to blame for a large percentage of the medical problems faced by society today, and once again the principle effect is to cause congestion in the body. However, in this case the congestion is primarily caused in the heart, which results in the same decrease in energy because of the same kind of compromise in the body's ability to efficiently deliver oxygen.

And from there we could go on for a very long time about the importance of eating a balanced diet and being careful with what you eat and drink, but if your lifetime's worth of listening to lessons about the Word of Wisdom hasn't convinced you of the importance of taking better care of yourself, then my poor words in that respect aren't likely to have much of an impact either. So, let's go back to where we started and once again talk about the spiritual impact of not taking care of our physical bodies.

Think of the outrage you would feel if someone were to go into one of the temples and throw dirt and garbage up and down the halls of the building. Imagine your reaction to graffiti being sprayed on the walls outside, and consider your reaction to the desecration of one of the celestial rooms.

Then ask yourself this question: Why is it that I do not react the same way to the desecration of my own personal temple, and why don't I recognize and admit the corresponding withdrawal of the Spirit?

Is it possible that even as committed and participating church members we do not recognize the real impact of what we put into our bodies in terms of food and drink? I know that we do not have empirical data the equal of what Lance Armstrong had available to prove the impact of a two-week lay off, but are we so spiritually insensitive and naïve as to believe that there is no correlation? I greatly fear that we are.

But even after all of that, there is an even greater issue at hand. For yet again we have come back to what we think and feel about ourselves, and the corresponding impact that those thoughts and feelings have on how we live our lives. For as with everything else we have discussed under two different principle headings, I am convinced that our thoughts about ourselves are at the very core of how well or how poorly we take care of our physical bodies.

I know that some are genetically disposed to be taller and some shorter; some are designed to have bigger bones than others so as to support a larger amount of weight, and some are naturally small; but the single biggest factor in the horizontal growth of the American population is our utter refusal to take control of what and how much we put into our own mouths.

Why is this such an issue? For exactly the same reasons that addiction in all of its forms and the sexual issues previously discussed are. Because if "the spirit and the body are the soul of man" (D&C 88:15), that means that when we refuse to accept our responsibility to properly maintain our physical body we are also refusing to maintain our spiritual awareness. So, when we degrade ourselves physically in *any* fashion, the spiritual decline has to at least be equal to the physical. Once again, for every physical action or thought, there is an equal and corresponding spiritual reaction.

And does any of this mean that it is impossible to feel the Spirit when we both allow and speed our physical deterioration?

Obviously not. It only means that, in the same fashion as if we smoked or drank, we make the process far more difficult than we are aware of; and we do so because we are just as unaware of the spiritual consequence as are those who smoke and drink.

For in the same sense that the effects of physical decline are cumulative, the spiritual damage just keeps accumulating too. After all, have you ever talked to someone who has recently lost a significant amount of weight? You know, twenty or thirty pounds? In every case the first thing that you hear is how much better they *feel.* And if losing that relatively small amount of weight has that much impact on how a person *feels* physically, how magnified do you think the corresponding improvement in that person's ability to *feel* the Spirit is?

So, the physical decline associated with poor maintenance of our temple cannot be limited to the few items specifically prohibited by the Word of Wisdom, nor is the corresponding decrease in our spiritual awareness. It must be the same in all cases.

ADD, ADHD, depression, bipolar disorder, and any other mental health issue

At the beginning of this section I must state in the most emphatic terms possible that clinical depression, bipolar disorder, ADD and ADHD, psychosis, schizophrenia, and a host of other mental health diagnoses are real and provable brain-based conditions. Each of these can be diagnosed using modern brain scan technology, and diagnoses are made based on the specific areas of the brain affected by each. We are talking about conditions that can be proven as empirically as the effects of a two-week break in Lance Armstrong's training.

And as one who has lived my life with ADD, I can personally attest to the reality of the effects and far-reaching impact that any one of these conditions has on a person's life.

So, nothing that follows is intended to replace competent medical and psychological evaluation, nor do I believe that it is inappropriate to seek such help. In fact, I believe it is the height of foolishness not to seek such help.

And I can state just as emphatically, *nothing* has had a more positive impact on my ability to live my life with ADD than having a relationship with Father and the great blessing of having experiences with the Spirit as a part of my life.

To provide a spiritual diagnosis and a spiritual prescription for these conditions—and it must be noted that we're not just talking about the mental health conditions listed above, but about any mental health issue or thinking error that you want to include on your list—we turn to the last chapter of the Book of Mormon.

In the last chapter of the Book of Mormon—after Moroni gives the promise that we should know so well, and after a review of the gifts of the

Spirit—he gives us a critical insight about the effect of the withdrawal of the Spirit. He says, "Wherefore, there must be faith; and if there must be faith there must also be hope; and if there must be hope there must also be charity. And except ye have charity ye can in nowise be saved in the kingdom of God; neither can ye be saved in the kingdom of God if ye have not faith; neither can ye if ye have no hope. And if ye have no hope ye must needs be in despair; and despair cometh because of iniquity" (Moroni 10:20–22).

Could there ever be a better description of clinical depression than to say that someone suffering from that condition has "no hope"? If there is, I can't imagine what it might be. But Moroni is also using that term in a different context from the one that we usually think of. For when he talks of faith, hope, and charity, he is using those terms as specific references to Jesus Christ as our Savior and Redeemer. He is in fact saying that Jesus Christ must be the focus of our faith, hope, and charity.

So, as I live my life with ADD—or with addicted children, or with any other condition or thinking error you might want to name—whenever any of us find ourselves distracted from the things that bring us peace and happiness, indeed when we are in despair, we must always return to the following line of reasoning: If despair comes because of iniquity, are there specific forms of iniquity that are identified as the cause of that despair?

Yes, there are. The first thing Moroni tells us that we must have if we are to avoid despair is faith, but faith in what? The obvious answer to this question must always be Jesus Christ as our personal Savior and Redeemer.

Second, Moroni tells us that we must have hope, but hope of what? To this we must always answer, hope of a glorious resurrection and eternal salvation in and through the Atonement of Jesus Christ, for that is the message of his entire life!

Third, Moroni tells us that we must have charity, but what is charity? This answer must always be that true charity is the pure love of Christ, and of all mankind too.

If we are still in despair after we have the answers to these questions, the only possible conclusion is that our daily application of at least one of these principles is lacking in some fashion. It can only mean that we have—at least to some degree—lost our faith in Jesus Christ as our personal Savior, or that we have lost focus on our hope of a glorious resurrection and eternal salvation because of his life and Atonement, which also usually means that we have lost our love of Christ and all men.

I can only speak for myself, but after reviewing these questions in my mind, I find that I invariably feel much better about the situation, regardless of the issue involved. For I know in whom I have trusted, and I know that salvation comes only in and through the Lord Jesus Christ and his Atonement for each of us as individuals. I further know that a glorious resurrection awaits each of us, regardless of any action on our part, and I know that the same opportunities are available to all mankind and upon the same conditions.

So, get the best medical and mental health treatment that you have access to. Learn as much as you can about how your brain works and what you can do to improve your individual thinking; and at the same time recognize that "the Comforter . . . shall teach you all things, and bring all things to your remembrance" (John 14:26).

Notes

1. Boyd K. Packer, "Ye Are the Temple of God," in Conference Report, Oct. 2000.
2. MedicineNet, "Anorexia Nervosa," http://www.medicinenet.com/anorexia_nervosa/article.htm.

4.4 The End Results

THE ULTIMATE EXAMPLE OF THE EFFECTIVENESS OF THIS approach is to consider the healing miracles performed by the Savior during his earthly ministry. Most of the cases that we have a record of include some form of physical problem or deformity, and a good number of them also include mental health issues. In every case the Savior was able to instantly cure the problem, regardless of its origin or severity, which means that we must acknowledge his power to heal us in all three areas of our lives—physical, psychological, and spiritual. All we have to do is figure out how to tap into his healing power.

As a specific example of how well this process works, consider the story of a good friend. This man was a faithful member of the Church and served an honorable mission, but after his return home—and after a period of time had passed—he fell into the twin traps of drug addiction and the homosexual lifestyle. This behavior went on for over fifteen years, and it produced all of the attendant problems that are attached to that lifestyle. After all, what I like to refer to as The Laws of Natural Consequences are not man's laws; they are God's laws, and he is unyielding in his adherence to them. Not that he takes any pleasure in watching us suffer the consequences of our actions; in fact, just the opposite is the case. But because of his perfect understanding, he realizes that, at least from an eternal perspective, taking away the pain and suffering caused by our poor choices is the worst thing he could possibly do for us.

And so my friend was left to deal with the brutal reality of the loneliness, fear, self-doubt, physical decline, and spiritual emptiness that must accompany such choices.

It is painful to watch someone you respect so much in one part of his life struggle so mightily in many others. But as it is in virtually all cases, there was no other choice available, for until he recognized the destructive nature of his own thoughts, choices, and actions for himself, and until he came to the realization that he could only be made whole through the twin processes of repentance and change, the pain and suffering continued unabated.

But because Father is merciful to us all—regardless of our choices or lifestyle—and because a certain limited amount of spiritual guidance is available to us all—again, regardless of our choices or lifestyle—my friend was able to begin the repentance process.

I do not know how long it took—and it really doesn't matter. But what does matter is that he has since returned to full Church activity, married another dear friend of mine, and after having his temple blessings restored, has been sealed for time and all eternity in the temple of our God. He now serves on the high council of his stake and is working on a book of his own to further address these issues.

A few years ago, I asked him the following question: "It is such a massive change to move from that lifestyle back to full Church activity that there aren't very many who pull it off. How did you do it?"

His response was short and to the point. He simply said, "Alan, when you are open to the promptings of the Spirit, anything is possible."

I have never heard it said any better than that because it can't be said any better than that. And praise be to God that there are so many who have had the same experience in regards to so many different issues.

That is but one brief example from the many I know, and it should be sufficient to make the point for now, so let's move on again.

Principle Five

Parenting—Using the Lord as a Role Model

5.1 The Sin Be Upon the Head of the Parents?

A quick note to start with

This principle needs to start with a well-known, but new-to-us, approach to parenting that we have recently learned about through our child's treatment program.

This approach is called Parenting with Love and Logic, or Love and Logic for short. It has been around since the late seventies, and I wish with all my heart that we had learned of it when we first became parents. It is impossible to know the amount or kind of difference it would have made in our home, but I feel very safe in saying that had we known about it sooner we could have avoided at least some of the issues that we have been confronted with. Here is a quick summary of the ideas behind this parenting technique:

> Love and Logic is a philosophy of raising and teaching children which allows adults to be happier, empowered, and more skilled in the interactions with children. Love allows children to grow through their mistakes. Logic allows children to live with the consequences of their choices. Love and Logic is a way of working with children that puts parents and teachers back in control, teaches children to be responsible, and prepares young people to live in the real world, with its many choices and consequences.[1]

Outside of the scriptures, Love and Logic has more practical and realistic parenting instruction than anything else I am aware of, and it is impossible to recommend it too highly. A simple Google search will provide sufficient information as a starting point for your research.

Modern challenges

It is both comforting and critically important to acknowledge that there has never been a more difficult time in which to raise functional children than the one we now live in.

Just think of the magnitude of that statement. From Civil War times, when war began to be poured out upon all nations; throughout the Spanish Inquisition, the Dark Ages and the Crusades; back to the Meridian of Time when Christ walked the earth as a mortal man and the House of Israel was subjected to Roman domination; through the terror of the Ming Dynasty and the bloody conquests of Alexander the Great; all the way back to the initial enslavement of Israel, and even further back to the debauchery of Sodom and Gomorrah; even when considering all of those, this is still the most difficult time in all the long history of the world in which to attempt to raise reasonably functional children, let alone righteous ones.

How is it possible to accurately make such a statement? Because in all of the world's history, there has never been a time when it has been so easy for the adversary to distract our young people from the things that will bring them safety, security, and happiness. And for an additional perspective on these issues, we again turn to Arthur C. Clarke, who said, "Before you become too entranced with gorgeous gadgets and mesmerizing video displays, let me remind you that information is not knowledge, knowledge is not wisdom, and wisdom is not foresight. Each grows out of the other, and we need them all."

In what is probably the greatest example we will ever have of the eternal principle that everything has its opposite, the amazing technological advances of the last twenty-five years now make it possible for the Lord's chosen servants to be seen and heard simultaneously throughout most of the earth. It is now not only possible but easy for us to have access to entire libraries of spiritual thinking and knowledge from virtually any age, region, or religion of the earth. Those same technologies are also used to give that same easy access to an incomprehensible amount of degrading, demoralizing, destructive, and deadly information. Never in all the world have young people been so confronted with images and sounds specifically designed to distract them from the things of the Spirit, and never in all of eternity has there been a more precisely focused effort to turn children against their parents.

So please do not underestimate the magnitude of the challenge that we face. But as Elisha was told, "Fear not, for they that be with us are more than they that be with them" (2 Kings 6:16).

"The sin be upon the heads of the parents" (D&C 68:25).

Of all the feelings that have and will come from watching our children struggle so mightily, none can be more physically, emotionally, and spiritually debilitating; none can cause more hurt and pain; none can create more long-term problems for everyone involved; and none is more inappropriate and misguided than those created when we blame ourselves for the actions and choices of our children. Yet it is completely natural for us to do so, and it also seems to be in harmony with the scripture quoted above.

I can also understand if right about now you are thinking, *Come on Alan. You are now in direct contradiction with the scriptures, and if you don't make some serious changes in your thinking, and very quickly too, then I'm finished with your little book!* As well you should be if such were the case.

So let's take a little more in-depth look at what section 68 actually says about our responsibilities as parents:

> And again, inasmuch as parents have children in Zion, or in any of her stakes which are organized, that teach them not to understand the doctrine of repentance, faith in Christ the Son of the living God, and of baptism and the gift of the Holy Ghost by the laying on of the hands, when eight years old, the sin be upon the heads of the parents. . . .
>
> And their children shall be baptized for the remission of their sins when eight years old, and receive the laying on of the hands.
>
> And they shall also teach their children to pray, and to walk uprightly before the Lord. (D&C 68:25, 27–28)

After all my years of reading and pondering on those verses, I have yet to find any hint of the idea that we are responsible for the actions of our children. But what we do find stated very clearly is the fact that we are responsible for teaching our children correct principles. These verses plainly state that Father will hold us accountable for what we teach our children, but there is no mention made of our accountability for what they do with those teachings.

Because it so very clearly states, "The sin be upon the heads of the parents," there can actually be a time when we are called to account for our children's actions, so when is that time? It will only come if we do not teach them faith, repentance, baptism, and the laying on of hands when eight years old, and only if we fail to continue teaching those same principles throughout their lives; only if we say, "But they are so stubborn and headstrong, and there is nothing I can do to prevent their behavior." In short, only if and when we give up and stop trying will we be held in any way responsible for the choices of our children.

As our challenges have intensified over the years, there have been several times that my dear wife has looked at me and said something to the effect of, "I'm the one who stayed home with them; I'm the one who provided most of their instruction and training; I'm the one they spent the most time with; so it must be that their actions come about because of my inadequacies and mistakes." In short, she has been under the false impression that it's all her fault.

We have had unnumbered conversations about this specific issue, and I have used the following analogy on multiple occasions. It has taken several years, but in recent months I believe not only that the reality of this analogy is clear to her, but that she now takes great comfort from it.

For of all the great truths thus far revealed about the fullness of the gospel, none can provide more perspective than the fact that God is the literal Father of our spirits, that he knows each of us as a separate spirit, and that he is personally interested in the course of our individual lives. Back under the heading of Principles One and Two we examined his involvement in presenting the plan of salvation to us all, and we also learned of his awareness of the choices we each made in relation to that plan. This can only mean that he was and is a parent in exactly the same sense that we are. For further clarification of this concept, please consider this quote:

> We are the children of God, and as His children there is no attribute we ascribe to Him that we do not possess, though they may be dormant or in embryo. The truth is that God is our Father, and we are His children. What a tender relationship! What a feeling of nearness it creates within us! What? God my Father? Am I indeed His son? Am I indeed His daughter? Do I belong to the Family of God? Is this literally true? The answer is "Yes." God has revealed it, that we are literally His children, His offspring, that we are just as much His children as our offspring are our children, that He begot us, and that we existed with Him in the family relationship as His children.[2]

There is great comfort in these realizations for me, and I find tremendous peace in the fact that Father has dealt with rebellious children on a far grander scale than I have. I find even greater comfort in the knowledge that though he is perfect in everything he does—especially in his teaching of all those present in the premortal existence—he lost one third of the host of heaven before the world was even created.

And how could that possibly happen when you have a perfect teacher? Simply because of the eternal principle of agency. So in other words, we just *think* our child is the devil. His child actually is.

Is there a perspective there that you might not have considered before? And if you have, has it been that explicit? And does that perspective—the fact that God has a child who is the father of all lies, the fact that he has a multitude of children who are in direct opposition to everything good and holy that he stands for, and yet Father remains perfect and the giver of all good gifts—give you hope enough to carry on through whatever trials might come your way? Or do you merely struggle with the idea that—just as you do—your children have the absolute right to self-determination?

A close friend of mine probably expressed it best when he first heard the general subject of this book. He said, "If I were to write that book the title would have to be *Free Agency and How to Enforce It.*"

We had a good laugh at the comment, and as a former bishop he fully understands the futility of that approach. But there is nothing at all humorous about actually taking that approach with our children. Yet that is the approach that is taken all too frequently.

Notes

1. Love and Logic Institute, "Frequently Asked Questions," URL http://www.loveandlogic.com/faq.html.
2. George Q. Cannon, *Gospel Truth*, vol. 1 (Salt Lake City: Deseret Book, 1987), 1.

5.2 God Our Father
Examining His Approach to Parenting

EVERYTHING THAT FOLLOWS—IN FACT EVERYTHING IN the entire book—is based on a psychological concept called behavior modeling. Or is behavior modeling really a spiritual principle that is best expressed as, "He that believeth on me, the works that I do shall he do also" (John 14:12)? Sometimes I have a hard time telling the two apart.

Either way, the result is the same. And that result is that when there is a particular skill that we want or need to develop, the quickest and most efficient way to develop that skill is to find someone who already does it well, learn everything we can—we're talking about very specific details here—about how they do it, and then determine how we can best repeat that process. A few common examples would be any form of teacher-student, coach-athlete, boss-employee, parent-child relationship. Oh, wait. I just said that our role model should be someone who already does the skill well. Sorry, I must be getting ahead of myself again. (It's really hard to write as sarcastically as I talk when I say something like that, so I hope you got the point.)

I'm hoping that when you read it that way, you will think back to Principle Three and do a quick mental review of the idea that our behavior happens in repeatable patterns, and that if you can figure out *how* you learned to do something the way you do, that means you can also learn how to do it differently. That's why we spent so much time on those concepts in the first place. But when we talk about modeling our approach to parenting on the same methods that Father uses with us, it should go without saying that we need to make sure we understand what those methods really are. So let's see if we can learn a few things about parenting by examining the Father's approach.

Meet them where they are.

Of all the mistakes that we mortals make as parents, few will ever match the problems caused by the twin traps of having idealized and unrealistic expectations of our children's capabilities. You know, exactly like what would happen if Father expected us to perform at his level of perfection without the experiences and insights provided by mortality.

Just imagine what would happen if he expected us to both live and understand as he does, without our having had these experiences. After all, he really is perfect, and there is nothing he does not know, so imagine the difficulty we would have in meeting his standard of living, without having these experiences on which to base our choices and decisions. I hope I'm not the only one thinking that sounds impossible. Yet how many times do we expect our children to make better decisions than are appropriate for their current level of development?

And here is some really scary news for you: In the last few years it has been conclusively proven that the frontal lobes of our brain—unfortunately that's the part that is responsible for logical and rational thinking—aren't fully developed until around age twenty-five. As support for that statement, please consider this quote: "A National Institutes of Health study suggests that the region of the brain that inhibits risky behavior is not fully formed until age 25."[1]

Imagine that. Total justification for a sentiment expressed by virtually every parent of a teenager in the history of the universe: "There must be something wrong with your brain for you to think and act the way you do!"

Of course, there is a minor problem with that line of thinking. Or have you forgotten that you were once a teenager too? Have you conveniently chosen not to remember what a wonderful experience those years were for you? Notice that I didn't say you forgot, only that you chose not to remember. There are many who are like my dear wife and have made very few poor choices in their lives, but I think the point is pretty obvious too. Given my sterling record of perfect decision-making, what could ever make me think that my children would do any better job of dealing with that process than I did?

Please learn to accept the fact that—just like you—your children are not perfect, and they aren't going to be perfect any time soon either. Learn to live with the reality that—again, just like you—they are doing the best they know how to do, and the bad decisions they make are based on the information and experience that *they* have available. You further need to come to grips with the fact that even when they are making life-threatening decisions, any time you try to impose your beliefs, attitudes, and understandings upon them they will fight you at every turn. And most important of all, never forget whose plan it still is to get you to try to force them into conforming their behavior to your will.

I can hear it now: "But Alan, you don't understand. My kid has four earrings in her ear, and the prophet said . . ." Oh, I understand. We've been through that one too, except it was only one earring, and it was in my son's ear. When that one happened I had multiple extended family members ask me how I could allow such a thing.

How could I allow such a thing? This may sound overly simplistic, but what other choice did I have? Oh yes, I could have ripped it from his ear as was suggested by more than one family member, but what purpose would that have served? What would have been accomplished other than building a giant wall between my son and myself, and when far worse things began to develop just a little further down the road, what kind of influence could I have had then?

So I fulfilled my obligation as detailed in section 68 and explained the Lord's standard as expressed by President Hinckley. My son was taught the correct principle and left to exercise his agency and make the decision of whether or not to leave it in. After all, it's his life, and once I have taught the correct principle, he is the one who will be held accountable for what he does with that knowledge. Furthermore, since Father is willing to cut me so much slack in my own life, why would I not allow my children the same opportunity? You know, why would I expect them to make better decisions than I did when I was their age?

And given the myriad contradictory and dissenting viewpoints that young people are bombarded with in today's world, what could possibly lead me to believe that they would make even as many good decisions as I did? After all, is it easier now than it was thirty-five years ago, when I was a teenager? If the answer is a resounding no—and there can be no question that it is—then why do we expect more of our children than Father expects of us?

It must also be noted that one of the things Father never does during this process is lower the standards of what is acceptable based on our performance. By now it should be obvious that it is contrary to the order of heaven for him to do so because if he did we could not then be raised to his level of perfection; he could only be lowered to our level of imperfection.

So maintain your own standards and righteous conduct while allowing your children to determine their own approach to those same standards.

"A soft answer turneth away wrath."

The full quote from Proverbs is, "A soft answer turneth away wrath: but grievous words stir up anger. The tongue of the wise useth knowledge aright: but the mouth of fools poureth out foolishness" (Proverbs 15:1–2).

And here's another little gem from the previous chapter of Proverbs: "He that is slow to wrath is of great understanding: but he that is hasty of spirit exalteth folly" (Proverbs 14:29). Sadly, I have exalted far too much folly as a parent for I am far too "hasty of spirit."

I know I am not the first to make this observation, but the coarsening of the dialogue in modern society, and the volume at which that dialogue takes place, are causes for major alarm. It may be an overstatement, but probably not much of one, to say that there are very few things that cause more problems in modern society than the language that passes for acceptable conversation and the volume at which it takes place. Our world is also full of people who perfectly match a description from Isaiah as those "that make a man [or a child] an offender for a word" (Isaiah 29:21).

But what is Father's method of dealing with us when we make mistakes? Does he belittle us and repeatedly remind us of every mistake we have ever made, or does he meet us where we are and then offer to help us improve our behavior. Does he scold us when we make the same mistake over and over again, or does he accept our efforts at improving our behavior, recognize the difficulty of the task, and give us the credit we deserve for our efforts at improvement? Regardless of the offense involved, has he ever refused to listen to you, or is he always available?

I can only speak for myself, but my experience is that as long as I am honest in my acknowledgment of my actions and in my willingness to accept responsibility for them, as long as I am sincere in my desire to repent, Father is always there to put his arm around me and give me the encouragement and help that I need. Not that he is happy with me when

I do something foolish—and I have found him to be especially unhappy when I repeat the same negative behavior multiple times—but he has never turned me away, and he has never, ever given me the impression that all is lost and there is no hope of a reconciliation.

It has also been my experience that even though I have seriously disappointed him at times; even though there have been times when my behavior has not been in line with my knowledge of his will; even though he has been mightily frustrated with me and there have been occasions of "reproving betimes with sharpness" (D&C 121:43); he has never left me "comfortless" (John 14:18), and he has always been anxious to enter whenever I am willing to open the door (see Revelation 3:20).

Further, as my understanding has been influenced by our challenges over these many years, I have found that the following thought process helps me to maintain a less confrontational perspective.

During the Sermon on the Mount, the Savior said, "Judge not, that ye be not judged" (Matthew 7:1). It is unfortunate that these words are so often used in a misguided attempt to justify poor choices, and even more unfortunate that we so seldom read the footnote from the Joseph Smith Translation that clarifies the need for—and in fact requires—appropriate and righteous judgment.

But the real power of this part of the sermon actually comes from verse 2, where it says, "For with what judgment ye judge, ye shall be judged: and with what measure ye mete, it shall be measured to you again" (Matthew 7:2). As we have dealt with wayward children I have found it beneficial to ask myself how well I measure up to the standard that I am asking of them. I have found this to be important because even as we have been confronted with some very poor decisions, it gives me an awareness of the need to remember my own shortcomings and to temper my reactions accordingly. Not that we haven't had some monumental blow-ups in our home, but given what we have been through I think they have been less frequent than you might imagine. And I know that they have been far more frequent than I like to remember too.

The real point is that because I am so far from perfect myself, I need to be very careful with the standards and expectations that I try to hold my children to. So if you want to maintain any semblance of an ongoing relationship with your children, speak softly and carefully when things don't go the way you want them to. Which brings us to our next topic.

Words matter a lot—and so do other things.

George Bernard Shaw, one of the great writers and communicators of all time, once said, "The biggest problem with communication is the illusion that it has been accomplished." Seldom have truer or more accurate words been spoken. And why is interpersonal communication so difficult? Because you live in your head and I live in mine. Because you know what you mean when you use a particular word or phrase, but because your experiences are not mine, those words and phrases do not mean the same thing to me that they do to you; they are not represented the same way in my head that they are in yours. So we are, once again, forced to acknowledge the fact that there are far too many times that our communications are a "best guess" experience, meaning that we each do the best we can to interpret the other person's meaning based on our own experience and understanding. But what are the tools we use to make such an interpretation?

There are three components involved in any communications experience:

1. Words themselves—the actual words spoken by both parties in a conversation
2. Voice inflection and intonation—the way you say what you say
3. Body language—what you say with the rest of your body

There was research published back in the early seventies that stated that words themselves account for less than 10 percent of the communication experience, with intonation and inflection at about 35 percent and body language at almost 55 percent. Those statistics have been widely quoted for nearly forty years now and deserve at least a brief mention in any discussion about this issue. But since practical application is our real goal, let's take a slightly different approach.

How many different meanings can you give to the word *yes* with just a different tone of voice? How about *no*? If we were just interested in making a list of descriptors, it could well take the rest of the book to finish that list, but the more obvious point is that how you say what you say has a huge impact on the message being sent and—of far greater importance—on how it's received too.

And if you would like a graphic example of the messages carried by body language alone, consider those whose only method of communication is sign language. Kind of the ultimate body language, don't you think? They may not be able to vocalize words, but if you watch them communicate, you know that all of the emotions, inflections, and passion are just as present as in spoken conversation.

So using these thoughts as a reference point, consider what it's like for your acting-out teenager when you get right in his face with your own face bright red, veins bulging in your neck and forehead, finger pointed directly at his chest, and then you go on a five-minute tirade. You know the kind I'm talking about: lots of personal put downs, lots of sarcasm, lots of anger, eyes flashing, voice pounding like a drum, emotions running out your ears.

Or am I the only one who has ever done that?

Now imagine what it was like for that same child the first time a scene like that was played out for them. That child was what, two or three months old? And even if it never happened until the kid was two or three years old, imagine the impact of that much raw emotion being dumped into their brain. Maybe you don't have to imagine it at all, because in the real world it is almost guaranteed that the exact same thing happened to you when you were that young. Those are some pretty frightening memories, right?

Then when you revisit the concepts of how we learned our behaviors in the first place, and how that learning becomes a repeatable pattern, I hope this last description sheds some light on the doctrine that God will visit "the iniquity of the fathers upon the children unto the third and fourth generation" (Deuteronomy 5:9). And we wonder how and why it is that we end up turning into our parents. So give your kids a break and get out of their face for a while, and remember Einstein's comment about needing to do something different if you want to get a different result.

Notes

1. Elizabeth Williamson, "Brain Immaturity Could Explain Teenage Crash Rate," *Washington Post*, February 1, 2005.

5.3 Shoulder-to-Shoulder Parenting

AFTER NINE YEARS OF WHAT I HAVE SOMETIMES referred to as "combat parenting"—meaning that we have been fighting the battle on a daily basis, and against some of the most dreaded foes that any of us can ever face—I state without hesitation that this approach has had a more positive impact on our efforts as parents than any other single thing we have done. As such, it is almost impossible to overstate the impact that an understanding of what follows can have on your life and family.

And I hear you question: "But, Alan, if it is so critically important, why didn't it show up earlier in the section?" My answer is that we needed to have the other thinking concepts in place before attempting to explain this approach. Why, you ask? Because while these ideas are easy to explain, they are very difficult to implement, and you need to have as many different thinking approaches available as you possibly can. Why, again? Because having more information, having lots of different approaches in mind, increases the potential for success. But don't kid yourself; what follows may be an even bigger trial than dealing with wayward children.

Shoulder-to-shoulder parenting simply means that as parents you must be willing to stand shoulder to shoulder with your spouse through whatever comes your way. It means that you must communicate well enough with each other that your children cannot play one against the other and manipulate circumstances to their advantage. It simply means that you must have the same kind of unity with your spouse that Father has with our elder brother.

Only now do you understand the magnitude of the challenge.

And to those who are single parents, do not despair. While I cannot begin to imagine the difficulty of raising children while alone in today's world, I firmly believe the message this scripture has for you: "Keep all the commandments and covenants by which ye are bound; and I will cause the heavens to shake for your good, and Satan shall tremble and Zion shall rejoice upon the hills and flourish; . . . Fear not, little flock, the kingdom is yours until I come" (D&C 35:24, 27). But how is such a thing to be accomplished in such a diverse and troubled world?

Once again, we need to expand our understanding of what Father does, for of all the Godly attributes involved in the parenting process it seems to me that these two are absolutely paramount: consistency in all things and application of consequences.

The importance of consistency

It has been observed by an amazing array of different teachers, counselors, and therapists that what children want and need more than any other thing in life is consistency. The best way I have ever heard it said is by Dr. Phil McGraw, for whom this statement almost amounts to a mantra: "Children need to be able to predict the consequences of their behavior with 100 percent accuracy."

After reading that statement, you need to do a quick mental review of the concept of Father as a perfect being, one whose behavior and responses can be predicted with 100 percent accuracy. (And does that make it even clearer why we spent so much time establishing that fact back in the chapters of Principle One?) Then you need to ask yourself how you are doing in that regard, and of far greater importance, you must consider the impact that it has on your children when you do not follow that model.

Does putting the issue in that form, and does stating it that pointedly, help you to understand the perspective involved? Does making a direct comparison between the way Father parents you and the way you parent your children create a bit more receptive mind-set? Does this explanation help you to recognize the great gift that it is, and do you recognize the freedom that it makes available to our children, when we follow eternal principles in everything we think, do, and say, rather than being "children, tossed to and fro, and carried about with every wind of doctrine, by the sleight of men, and cunning craftiness, whereby they lie in wait to deceive" (Ephesians 4:14)?

Are you beginning to recognize the critical need of meeting your children where they are? Do you understand the need to change some of your parenting techniques, and the importance of not just blindly following the track laid out before you by your parents as you may have done in the past? Do you recognize the fallacy of falling back on "that's just the way I am" thinking, and do you now recognize that approach as an abrogation of the agency that makes accountability and salvation possible in the first place?

Hard questions, all. But not nearly so hard as the ones we will face if we do not learn how to apply the answers in our own lives.

I can understand a healthy skepticism in your reactions to these ideas. After all, with my track record, who am I to ramble on and on about what works and what doesn't? But then, our family's story isn't finished yet either.

The power of consequences

It may seem a bit strange to begin this part of our discussion with a question, but we are going to do so because I find that this one question puts the entire matter into a very proper perspective. Here it is: When was the last time that Father took away the consequence of even one of your poor choices? See? Case closed. Now we can move on. But not really, because, as usual, there is much more to it than that. I hope your immediate reaction is that the next time such a thing happens will be the first time, and I hope that reaction is based on the realization that to be God in the first place he must apply all of his laws and commandments with 100 percent consistency.

Now take a second to consider the level of consistency generally exhibited in today's world. At the most basic level—in our homes—do we see any consistency in the application of consequences, or is the attitude more often than not "It doesn't matter what I do; they are going to do whatever they want to—so why even try?" Because of the difficulty of the task, do we just give in and give up?

There is also the other common approach: "It's my way or the highway, and I'll beat you into compliance if I have to." Then we must ask ourselves if either of these approaches resembles what Father does in any way. If not, it is probably not a good idea to continue using either of them.

I know, I know, much easier said than done. But that's why we are here together in the first place, isn't it? So let's examine a scriptural example of how Father does it and then take a look at how a couple of prophets dealt with their own foolish children.

The parable of the prodigal (Luke 15:11–32)

Nowhere in scripture do we have a better description of the way Father deals with us than in the parable of the prodigal son. In this parable the father represents God and the two sons represent us as his children. There are two sons because ultimately there are only two types of behavior possible, meaning that we either follow after God and keep his commandments, or we don't.

We should all be familiar with the story of how one son was faithful and obedient to his father, and how the other asked for his inheritance and left home to live a life in direct opposition to the things his father had taught him. We should also remember that the prodigal spent his time and money in riotous living, breaking every commandment he could and throwing away his inheritance in the process.

If it has been a while since you read the parable, the reference was included above so that you can refresh your memory. As you read, keep the following questions in mind:

- Was it possible for the father to deny the request of his son? If so, why didn't he?
- Did the father go looking for his son in an attempt to lessen the impact of the consequences that came as a natural result of his choices? If not, why not? (In modern parlance it's referred to as helicopter parenting when we swoop in to save our children from their foolish choices.)
- Did the father begin the process of repairing the relationship with his son? If not, why not? Is it even possible for him to do so?
- What was the father's reaction when his son returned and admitted his foolishness? Did he berate him and send him on his way, or did he welcome him with open arms and forgive his foolishness?
- When the faithful son questioned his father's actions, what was he taught concerning his place in his father's heart and home?

As you reread the parable and consider these questions, I hope you are also developing your own list. I hope you realize that my questions come from my very individual circumstances, that my answers can only have a very general application in your life, and that you need to figure out the specific answers to your own situation for yourself. After all, if getting all the answers was just about reading a book, we already have the scriptures to turn to, and why would we then need apostles and prophets to reveal additional information and new truth based on today's needs?

We also have the examples of the prophets Alma and Mosiah and their approach to dealing with wayward children. We are told that "the sons of Mosiah were numbered among the unbelievers" and that Alma the Younger "became a very wicked and an idolatrous man. And he was a man of many words, and did speak much flattery to the people; therefore he led many of the people to do after the manner of his iniquities. And he became a great hindrance to the prosperity of the church of God; stealing away the hearts of the people; causing much dissension among the people; giving a chance for the enemy of God to exercise his power over them" (Mosiah 27:8–9).

Then a short time later, when confronted by an angel from the presence of the Father, Alma heard words that should give great hope to the parents of those who struggle so terribly because of the iniquity of today's world. The angel said, "Behold, the Lord hath heard . . . the prayers of his servant, Alma, who is thy father; for he has prayed with much faith concerning thee that thou mightest be brought to the knowledge of the truth; therefore, for this purpose have I come to convince thee of the power and authority of God, that the prayers of his servants might be answered according to their faith" (Mosiah 27:14).

So Alma and Mosiah, even though they were prophets, did the only thing they could do. They did the only thing—based on the eternal law of agency and the absolute right to self-determination—available to them. They fasted and prayed and pled with the Lord that he would help their children recognize the error of their ways and begin the repentance process. That their prayers were answered in such miraculous fashion is an interesting side note, but it is specific to their individual circumstance, for in virtually all cases Father leaves it to what I again refer to as the Laws of Natural Consequences to be the angel that calls both us and our children to repentance.

Those laws may not be as impressive as the appearance of an angel, and it may take very large amounts of pain and suffering before the lights come on and the lessons are learned—*and the lessons may not be learned in this lifetime*—but the Laws of Natural Consequences are brutally efficient teachers.

5.4 God's Law in the Natural World

IT HAS BEEN OBSERVED THAT WE LIVE IN AN "EAT WHAT you kill" world, and one of the great tragedies of our modern world is that we have become so disconnected from the examples of God's laws that exist in the natural world all around us. I'm specifically referring to what is commonly described as Survival of the Fittest or Natural Selection. While it is true that the scriptures are our primary source of information about Father, his nature, and laws, these are not the only method he has made available to us to assist in the learning process. Consider the following story, by an unknown author, entitled "Two Wolves":

> An old Cherokee chief was teaching his grandson about life.
>
> "A fight is going on inside me," he said to the boy. "It is a terrible fight, and it is between two wolves. One is evil—he is anger, envy, sorrow, regret, greed, arrogance, self-pity, guilt, resentment, inferiority, lies, false pride, superiority, self-doubt, and ego. The other is good—he is joy, peace, love, hope, serenity, humility, kindness, benevolence, empathy, generosity, truth, compassion, and faith. This same fight is going on inside you—and inside every other person too."
>
> The grandson thought about it for a minute and then asked his grandfather, "Which wolf will win?"
>
> The old chief simply replied, "The one you feed."

If you had already had the experience of watching two wolves fight, this little story would probably be a more effective way of helping you understand the nature of the inner conflict that goes on within each of us than all of the reading you went through in Principles Three and Four.

But have you ever seen two wolves fight? How about bears or lions, hippos or gorillas, orcas or sharks?

Is there a more thrilling sound in all of nature than when a big bull elk lays his head back and bugles his challenge to a rival? Have you ever watched one of those big bulls come crashing through a stand of trees with his head laid back, the eye tines of his rack snapping inch-thick branches like match sticks? And even if you have seen footage of any of these, it's pretty hard to understand the ferocity of such an experience without being there firsthand.

But have you ever considered the idea that we might be able to learn something about parenting by observing how it is done in the natural world? And if you have, do you watch mammals for that information or do you watch reptiles and insects? I would suggest that the animal world can teach us some very correct principles about proper parenting.

Isn't it interesting that contrary to the image that many hold of them, few mothers in all of nature are more caring and attentive than a grizzly bear or a lioness? These fierce predators watch over their cubs with a level of devotion and care that many a human parent would do well to emulate, and their commitment to teaching those cubs the skills necessary to survive in a difficult and hostile world is absolute. They will also defend them to the death against any and all that threaten them.

But what is interesting is the manner in which the cubs of both species find out it is time to move on with their lives. In the case of the bears, when the cubs have reached a certain age, and when the time comes for mother to have another litter, Mom withdraws her affection, sends the cubs on their way, and leaves them to make it on their own. This is accomplished in a simple but confusing manner, at least to the cubs.

When the time is right, in the same manner she would do if there were some kind of danger in the area, Mama bear simply chases the cubs up a tree and then turns and sprints in the other direction. They have had this experience many times before, and it would appear that nothing out of the ordinary is happening. But when Mama hasn't come back after about half an hour, the cubs start calling to her to find out if it is safe to come down. They don't know anything is different yet, so they stay in the tree but continue bawling to her to make sure it's safe. This process can go on for over an hour, but eventually the cubs figure out that something is different and Mama isn't around anymore.

So they come down out of the tree and into a completely different world, one where Mama isn't around to kill food for them anymore, and one where if they are going to survive they will have to use all of the skills she taught them in a practical and successful manner.

How do they realize the reality of their situation? It's not complicated. They get hungry and figure out that they either need to kill something or starve to death. Remember what I said about the Laws of Natural Consequences being brutally efficient teachers?

But what about the lions? How does it happen in their world? Because they stay with the family group beyond the time when they are expected to be self sufficient, the process is a little different for lion cubs. In this case, and when Mama lion knows the time is right for each individual cub, one of the kids will come for a little love and affection and simply get smacked upside the head for their trouble. That's right, Mama gives them a good cuff and basically says, "Okay, things have changed, and it's time for you to start contributing around here."

But Junior doesn't understand and comes back for more. So Mama smacks him another good one. From there the process repeats itself until the cub gets the message, decides it's time to eat, and joins in the next hunting party to start making a useful contribution to the family. In the case of female lion cubs, they stay with the family pride in a female-dominated environment and continue association with their mother on a more or less equal footing. Now both are responsible to provide food for everyone in the group, and the daughter will soon have cubs of her own to raise.

But it's a little different for the males. They will stay with the family group only so long as they are not a threat to the two males who lead that pride. As soon as they begin to mature and have the potential to be a physical threat to the family leaders, they are either forced out of the group or a dominant male kills them. Once again, brutally efficient.

But how does all of this apply to human parenting, you ask? Which brings us to some very personal examples.

5.5 Personal Examples

AS OUR CHILDREN REACHED THEIR TEEN YEARS, WE HAD many of the same general issues to deal with that you have. There was the same difficulty with general attitude and demeanor that is faced with virtually all children; the same issues over music, clothes, friends, TV programs, hairstyles, and countless others, just as you have probably had. Or will yet have.

All of these were expected to one degree or another, at least by me. I remembered my own teen years well enough to realize that there were going to be some bumps in the road, but what I wasn't ready for was the magnitude of the damage already done to the road prior to us getting there. I only say that as another comment on the general world we live in and on the omnipresence of influences far beyond any of our control. As such, it is impossible to overstate the magnitude of the negative influence of popular culture and media on all of our children, and as those forces continue their decent into that special kind of madness that only the adversary can approve of, it is also impossible to calculate the damage yet to be done.

I know, not a pretty picture. What follows isn't very pretty either. But if it helps even one of you to deal with the same challenges, then it's well worth the effort.

Where it begins

As we have talked extensively with our kids in an attempt to understand more about why they have made the choices they have, we have learned that in their minds there are three main reasons why these things happened:

- Peer pressure or basic need for acceptance, sometimes family generated
- Simple curiosity or boredom
- Not knowing how to stop, or if it was even possible to stop

We have been told that experimenting with illegal drugs began because of the first two reasons listed. And while the enormous influence of friends and the need for peer approval are at least semi-recognized, the added influence of curiosity and boredom are seldom taken into account. I also believe that those specific issues are drastically underestimated, and after extensive discussion I believe that it was a roughly fifty/fifty proposition as to which was more influential in our case.

When we found drug paraphernalia in our home for the first time it was a devastating shock, but it also explained most of the behavior changes that we had witnessed over a period of just a few months. There were the to-be-expected angry confrontations, along with the even more to-be-expected angry denials. There was a tightening of privileges, with much closer monitoring of behavior patterns. The consequences for poor choices and behavior were defined with great specificity, and those same consequences were administered as precisely as possible. We had multiple conversations—at least a thousand of them if you ask our kids—as a family in an attempt to increase the awareness of the danger involved. And all of them lasted for at least three hours. (Okay, more than once did they drag on for two hours or more, and that is probably my single worst mistake as a parent.) But we did the best we knew how to do in trying to deal with this kind of problem for the first time.

Using drugs began for the first time during this child's senior year of high school. Completing schoolwork and following through on basic assignments had been a struggle for Kelly ever since elementary school. She started sluffing classes on a daily basis and stopped doing homework altogether, yet a B grade was the lowest score on any test. With no preparation or study at all, she obtained a score of twenty-three on the ACT yet did not graduate from high school until six years after the rest of the class. In short, not only is this child not stupid or slow but exceptionally bright, to the point of being on the lower end of the genius IQ scale.

So the first major point for you to be aware of is that drug use and addiction are not just a problem for the less intelligent or less academically gifted. For in the exact same degree that Father is no respecter of persons or status, so it is with addiction in all its forms; addiction just happens to be at the opposite end of the behavior spectrum from the things of God, for there is no one less free than an addict.

The downward spiral

One of the most dangerous components of addiction is the well-known fact that addicts begin to spiral downward in all areas of their lives. What is less often realized or talked about is that the spiral is not only taking the addict down, down, down, but as the addiction deepens and the ability to reason and make rational choices deteriorates, the spiral accelerates at an ever increasing rate. Depending on the drug of choice—meth is at the top of this list—the acceleration can begin in just a few weeks, and the crash at the bottom of the spiral can be horrifyingly spectacular.

What causes this acceleration? Simply the withdrawal of the Spirit of God. Think Principle Four here if you have questions about this concept. Go back and look at the pictures again if you need a reminder of the magnitude of the problems associated with that kind of withdrawal.

And now, back to our story. Among the myriad things that we did not realize when we first discovered the drug use, worst of all was that in an attempt to offset the loss of self-esteem being caused by those activities, Kelly was openly bragging about these activities to siblings. We have been told that she did not actually advocate drug use, and I believe that to be the case, but it is also impossible to calculate the impact of such outrageous behavior on other children. It simply led the others to the top of the spiral.

We did the best we could, given our then-limited experience, to deal with the situation in a rational and positive manner. Standards and expectations were clearly defined—yet again—consequences for failure to comply were also again clearly defined, and we did everything we could to enforce those consequences. But addicts do not live in the rational world, so one of the first things you must realize when dealing with an addict is that you are not talking to them, you are talking to a drug-addled brain and a shell of the person you used to know. So do not expect anything rational or logical to come from an addict, for such things are beyond them.

As the experimentation continued, we were eventually dragged into the special hell that is methamphetamine. Because no other drug provides as high a high, full-on addiction to meth is common with the first use, and few drugs are as readily and cheaply available either. There are not strong enough words for the loathing I have for any addictive substance, but this one holds an especially dark place in my soul.

As things deteriorated over a period of a few months, there was increasingly bizarre behavior, which provoked unpleasant confrontations about those behaviors and attitudes. Kelly stayed away from home for ever longer periods of time, couch surfing began, and the kind of life that only those who live with and love an addict became our daily lot in life. And all the while we were being forced to deal with an ever-increasing list of the same kind of issues, problems, and confrontations as two of our other kids began their drug use.

It was also at this time, though none of our children were married, that we found out we were going to be grandparents. So it seems important to note that in the same sense that the birth of another child doesn't just add to the level of stress in a home, it creates a whole new stress, so it is with each of those who turns to the horrors of drugs and all of the problems associated with them. Thus, if you look up the word *stress* in the dictionary it says, "See Mangum family, 1998–"

The spiral accelerates

Because our first child to use drugs began at age seventeen, and because we were new to dealing with the problems associated with addiction, we didn't react in the way that we would now or that we have in subsequent cases. Not that we made the all-too-common mistake of minimizing the magnitude of the problem, but even given the things we did do, we were not as aggressive as we could, or probably should, have been.

All that really means is that we were still trying to use rational thinking and decision making as the blueprint for our approach. But once again, given the twin problems of a still-developing brain and having that same brain drastically compromised by drug use, such an approach has a less than zero chance of success.

So in this case, behavior deteriorated into a series of experiences with her either moving out of her own accord or being sent packing by us. Time away from our home ranged from a few days to three or four weeks, contact during these times was limited to non-existent. Most of the time we didn't know if or where she was eating or sleeping, and we never knew from one day to the next if or when there would be a knock at the door telling us that we needed to plan a funeral.

Each time she left there was always a request to return, with all of the required promises for improved behavior and attitudes quickly forthcoming. Because we were trying to apply the same pattern that Father does, we allowed the returns and did the best we could to provide the kind of environment that would make adherence to those promises not only possible, but also attractive.

Sadly, such choices are beyond the capacity of anyone involved in such activities, and the downward spiral continued at an ever-increasing rate.

Finally, after almost two years of this pattern repeating itself, we learned the full measure of degradation that the adversary is capable of leading someone to. For this is when we learned she had helped another sibling on the path to destruction by actually assisting in the process of injecting cocaine. The stated rational for such an action was, "Better to do it with someone who knows what they're doing. It's safer that way."

It was the ultimate betrayal for our family, and the last straw in this case. It was early spring of 2003 when this happened, and we sent our child packing for the last time.

Rock bottom

After leaving home, the downward spiral continued on for another year before the bottom came. Throughout this time our child always knew that our home was available for a shower or a meal, but that sleeping here and having a regular association with our family would not happen without a massive change in attitude and behavior. Summer and fall came and went with a contact every two to three weeks; we never knew when or if she was sleeping, eating, or bathing; and we knew nothing of job status, income, or what amounts and kinds of drugs she was using. We just knew that the situation was getting pretty grim.

Any conversations during this time were short, both in duration and on specifics, but such behavior is, unfortunately, to be expected when dealing with an addict. As fall turned into winter we were confronted with a reality that wouldn't be wished onto a dog, because it was starting to get cold and permanent lodging was simply not available.

Yet with the resourcefulness and desperation that only addiction can provide, she finally found an abandoned and deteriorating camper to sleep in.

As winter progressed, and as the desperation became enough to let us know it had been three to five days since the last meal, we would provide a meal at home and some food to last for a few days, and we also provided a sleeping bag and blankets to ward off the worst of the cold. Given the circumstances and attitudes involved, we were as supportive and positive as we could be without relenting and allowing her to move back in at home.

Finally in late February of 2004, things reached the critical point. She had lost significant weight, her health was deteriorating from the cold and all the drugs—specifically, it appeared that pneumonia was present in the lungs and respiratory system—and then the severe cold snap came. To this point it had been a fairly typical Utah winter, and we knew that even though the arrangement was far from ideal it was better than actually sleeping outside. In short, we knew that our child was not in imminent danger from the elements.

But when the weather forecast predicted sub-zero temperatures for most of a week we also knew that if she didn't get in out of the cold there was a better than fifty/fifty chance that we were going to be having a funeral.

So my dear wife got in the car and brought our child home. It was then, and will forever be, as tender and heartbreaking a scene as you can possibly imagine, for that kind of gratitude can only come from one who knows that their demise is imminent.

A rebound begins—for this one

The return home lasted for less than a week before the cold snap broke and temperatures rose back above zero. Which meant a few nights of warmth and consistent meals, a few nights of family association and loving contact, and a few days and nights of sobriety and sanity.

And then she was returned to the camper and dropped back off to deal with the brutal reality of the Laws of Natural Consequences.

Why, you ask? How could we be so cruel and heartless?

Simply because by then we knew to the depths of our souls that the only thing worse than those living conditions would be for us to take away the consequences of such actions. How so? Because doing so would have eliminated the opportunity to learn anything from those same experiences.

Further, I am convinced that had we done so an instant return to a life that is far worse than dying would have happened.

And then the first miracle came.

For only after all of that did our precious child wake up after just a few days more, look around and make a comparison between where she had been a few nights earlier and where she was—again—and finally come to the realization that the only thing needed to change those conditions was a change in attitudes and behavior, and a willingness to give up the drugs.

We had been down this road several times before, but something in Kelly's demeanor was different this time. Her level of defiance and anger was not the same, and we somehow knew that this time our child was serious. We also knew that the power of natural laws had finally made the point that if behavior did not change, she wasn't going to be around much longer.

So Kelly moved back into our home and the process of detoxification began.

If all you have personally experienced is addictive thinking or addiction to food, you can't begin to imagine how difficult it is to kick a raging drug addiction. The statistics that back that comment up are pretty grim too. Of the total population who enter some kind of rehab program, only one in three will make a complete recovery; the next third will have a reasonable degree of sobriety but will struggle to maintain that sobriety and stay away from their addictive behavior; and the final third will never be free of the daily struggle. Those who fall into this category, especially depending on the drug of choice, don't usually survive even to middle age. Between the overdoses, the drug related murders, and the actual suicides, it's a pretty ugly picture.

Yet Kelly's raging addiction to methamphetamine was left behind without a single visit to rehab, and if I never see another miracle in my lifetime this one is enough to give me the hope to carry on, regardless of how bleak the situation may be.

Parallel tracks

At this same time we had another child who was nearly eighteen years old and ready to graduate from high school. The drug of choice in this case was cocaine, but Chris somehow maintained regular school attendance and decent grades. In this case the drug use had been going on for over two years, with all of the same behaviors you read about before being added to our stress.

After seeing our absolute resolve to consistently apply consequences for poor choices—and with the added recognition that they would be applied without regard to the unpleasant nature of those consequences—Chris realized that graduation was only about three months away and that if there weren't a radical change in behavior it wouldn't be long until he was out in the camper too.

So another of our children was able to leave an addiction behind, again without a stint in rehab. He got very serious about saving money for a down payment on a car, and roughly ninety days later he graduated from high school with a B+ average and a car to call his own.

Finally, and sadly, at the same time we had sent Kelly packing, Riley was just getting started at the top of the cycle. This is the child that was sent to live with out-of-state relatives in an attempt to curb the drug use and get his behavior under control before things got completely out of hand. That was also the same fall and winter when Kelly was living in the camper, going through all of the unmitigated hell that has just been described.

So we had one living in an abandoned camper, one living out of state, and one just starting on the road to sobriety—all at the same time.

We made visits out of state every two to three weeks, talked on the phone every two to three nights, and stayed in as much contact as we thought was reasonable. After all, if we were always involved, what point was there in sending him to live in a different environment?

When Riley returned home the next spring, we had high hopes that the improvements we were seeing would be permanent. But because of the nature of addiction and addictive thinking—especially when those behaviors start in the early teen years—without a major intervention of some kind it is almost impossible to make permanent changes. We had hoped that being sent out of state would be such an intervention, but such was not to be the case.

So he returned to addictive behaviors, and the downward spiral commenced yet again. This time it took another year and a half before we had exhausted our new store of patience and ideas about how to deal with this situation. Because he was so much younger than the others when the spiral started to accelerate, his behavior was even more defiant and angry than what we had seen before. Riley often stayed out over a weekend with no calls or contact, and the lying and manipulation that we saw this time raised a bar that we didn't think it was possible to raise. So in this case, and after trying two other incremental steps first, we finally turned to the world of inpatient rehab and treatment.

It's now been a little over ten months since treatment began, and the results are nothing short of another miracle, for this time the change is even more dramatic. In fact, exposure to the treatment environment has been the catalyst for another sibling, Chris, to realize the danger posed by any form of addiction and to finally give up tobacco and alcohol altogether, at least for now. And if you think that statement is a little too pessimistic, it just means that you don't understand the one-day-at-a-time nature of addiction and the daily battle to maintain complete sobriety.

So the sun shines again in our world—at least on a more regular basis than it has for a very long time.

Where are we now

After being that open about the specifics of our challenges, it would be unfair of me not to give you a current update of our situation.

As of Thanksgiving 2006, we have one child who had been mostly clean and sober for about two and a half years. During that time this child graduated from high school and completed a two-year associate degree, has held a steady job throughout that time period, and, as was previously stated, was motivated to complete sobriety by the example of the sibling going through treatment. Complete sobriety has been maintained for about six months now, and the prognosis for ongoing sobriety looks as good as is reasonable to hope for, given the history involved. This child is planning on buying a home of their own and being completely on their own sometime in the spring of next year. We also hear that a return to college to complete a bachelors degree is also quite likely.

We have another who has struggled to maintain their sobriety. Thus far we are not aware of anything more than marijuana being used, but to modify an old saying from Alcoholics Anonymous, "Getting high once is too much and getting high a million times isn't enough." There is lots of work needed on this child's thinking and attitudes about being an addict, but we hold out great hope that the challenges will be recognized as an opportunity for learning and further development.

How will such development take place? The only way it can.

One day at a time.

Another child is struggling to figure out what they want from life. We all frequently make choices without realizing—or even considering—the long-term ramifications of our actions, and then when things turn out very differently than we thought they would, there is a major case of buyer's remorse. You know the thought: *This is not what I thought my life would be.* And so there is a constant battle for all of us to figure out where we fit in the world and what we really need to do to meet our own individual needs. Hopefully we can all gain the insight needed to carry on with our obligations in a way that will be positive for everyone involved.

And last but far from least, another child is progressing through the treatment program and we hope that there will be two graduations next year, one from treatment and one from high school. Graduating from high school would be a pretty major miracle by itself, but having eight months of sobriety on the ledger is an even greater accomplishment.

But that's only where things are today, and there are no guarantees that they will stay there for any longer than today. After all, it's a tough world out there, the adversary plays for keeps, and because of the eternal principle of agency, none of us are ever immune to major setbacks in our lives. All of which means that we are pretty much just like you are, proud of our children and their positive accomplishments and still very concerned for their well-being and long-term happiness. Our concerns may be over a little more dangerous issues than yours, but ours are ours and yours are yours, and each is just as valid as the other in their own environment.

Remember, "One person's hangnail, is another's severed limb."

And as unbelievable as it may sound, there are stories even more difficult for most to comprehend than what you have just read. There have been times over the years when my wife and I have said something to the effect of, "It can't get any worse," yet every time we have said that it has. But how could it get any worse than what I have already described, you ask?

To answer that question we must turn to two couples who are friends of mine and who have been through even more than we have. That statement is based on my own very subjective judgment of the situation; you will have to judge for yourself from what follows.

Couple number one has a child who is not only an addict, but has also been involved in other illegal activity under the guise of social activism. In addition to everything that you have read about with my family, this child has also been involved in property destruction that has lead to repeated run-ins with the legal system and, ultimately, prison time. As difficult as it would be to have to visit one of my kids in prison, for me personally it would be even more painful if their actions also had an impact on others, their property, and livelihoods.

These wonderful people have also had to deal with theft of their property to get the money needed to stay high. For whatever miraculous reasons, we have not had to deal with that specific problem.

And couple number two, after more than ten years of fighting the same battles you have already read about, finally had to bury their twenty-nine-year-old child after an overdose. So yes, until we have to bury a child, it can always get worse.

Moving on

What you have read here is a very condensed version of our lives over the last nine years. It must be so because, as you can imagine, the specific details are even more personal and graphic than what has been included here. But it would also be unfair of me not to include a short list of the warning signs that we have seen as our children's drug use began and escalated. We have not seen every one of these, but most have happened in our home. This list is included here to assist you in the process of early detection.

- Major changes in friends and associates. Do not down-play this one—it is a giant red flag.
- Separating parents from friends—another of the major signs. If they don't want you to know who they are with, it is because bad things are happening, *absolutely guaranteed.*
- Distancing from parents and family. Though this is a common teenage behavior, if you have not seen it and it starts to happen, it is a bad sign.
- Inbound phone calls with caller ID blocked or unavailable.
- Phone calls at all hours of the night. If they are high, they sure aren't sleeping.
- Rapid decline in school performance or attendance.
- Major changes in appearance—hair dyed black or multi-colored, all black clothing, dark or excessive makeup.
- Rapid weight loss—a major indicator of meth or heavy drug use, along with eating disorders.
- Frequently dilated eyes—one of the major indicators of meth use.

If the pupils don't contract when you shine a flashlight on them, it's almost guaranteed the individual is high.

- Eating disorders—these frequently go hand-in-hand with drug use in today's world.
- Self-mutilation.
- Lying and going to extremes to manipulate parents.
- Extreme mood swings. Mood swings are normal, but when they become an emotional roller coaster it's not a good sign.
- Anger and depression. If you haven't seen them before, you need to find out what's going on.
- If you ever hear, "My friends are my family," that is a dead giveaway.
- Running away—another major sign, because they are getting high and don't want to come home and be found out.
- Stealing from home to support the new habit—another dead giveaway. The first time it happens you know for sure what is going on.
- Loss of the ability to feel anything but despair and emptiness. Once again, go back and look at the pictures in Principle Four if you have any questions about what that looks like.[1]

Finally, and no matter how much they protest or try to guilt trip you out of it with things like "What's the matter? Don't you trust me?" you must have the courage to face reality and do a thorough search to make sure that there isn't drug paraphernalia or drugs somewhere in your home. This falls under the heading of doing whatever it takes, so don't let them intimidate you or guilt trip you into not following through.

Remember, you are literally fighting for their lives.

Notes

1. Alcoholics Anonymous, "The Twelve Steps of Alcoholics Anonymous," http://www.alcoholics-anonymous.org/en_services_for_members.cfm?PageID=98&SubPage=117.

Principle Six

"Be Still and Know that I Am God"

(D&C 101:16)

6.1 Enduring to the End, or Pressing Forward in Christ?

FROM THE HEADING TO D&C 101 WE READ:

> At this time the saints who had gathered in Missouri were suffering great persecution. Mobs had driven them from their homes in Jackson County, and some of them had tried to establish themselves in Van Buren County, but persecution followed them. The main body of the saints was at that time in Clay County, Missouri. Threats of death against individuals of the Church were many. The people had lost household furniture, clothing, livestock, and other personal property, and many of their crops had been destroyed.

Not a particularly pretty picture. But as is so often the case when trials come and we think that all is lost—and usually not until things are at their most difficult—the time comes when the God of Heaven sees fit to open the veil ever so slightly and give us a glimpse of the glory and majesty that are available to those who live in his presence.

So it was in the case of this revelation, and so it has been for my wife and me. One of the most important things I have had confirmed by our trials is how serious Father is about testing us to find out if we really mean it when we say that we want to return to live in his presence. At this point I don't know if I'm passing the test or not, but after everything we have been through thus far, I'd be a fool to give up and not see things through to their final conclusion.

So I guess the real question is, Where are you in your life? Are you simply trying to survive your challenges—you know, are you hanging on by your fingernails and just enduring to the end—or are you pressing forward in Christ with "a perfect brightness of hope" (2 Nephi 31:20)? And you thought all the hard questions had already been asked.

Do you recognize the difference between the two? Do you understand the personal power that comes to you from pressing forward and seeking after Christ and his glory, rather than "just" enduring, just gritting your teeth and getting through another minute, hour, or day? And no, I'm not saying that "enduring" is a bad thing, only that the attitude we endure with makes all the difference in our ability to learn from the daily experiences that life and our own choices bring our way.

By now I think you realize that as we have moved forward in our journey together, the questions and comments have gotten progressively more pointed and specific. That isn't going to change soon either, so this warning is that what follows in the early part of this chapter will be even more direct than anything you have read thus far. Though the comments referred to may sound familiar, please be assured that they are only intended to define a particular mind-set or thought pattern. As such, *they must not be interpreted as anything more than that.*

What do we teach?

In my thirty plus years of adult church activity, I have come to believe that no other religious organization on earth does a better job of teaching its members to keep the Lord's commandments than does The Church of Jesus Christ of Latter-day Saints. From our earliest days in Primary classes to our family home evenings to Young Women and Young Men activities to Seminary classes, we hear about keeping the commandments to the point that I fear it is the single best known and most often repeated admonition in all of our religious training and experience.

In the home, since we, as parents, have been baptized and confirmed members of the Church and are entitled to the presence of the Holy Ghost in our lives and homes, our children grow up in an environment where regular experiences with the Spirit of God are a reasonably common, if not frequent, occurrence. And what a great blessing it is that such is the case.

Then when they are baptized at the age of eight, hands are laid on their heads, and they are given the injunction to "receive the Holy Ghost" unto themselves. I can only speak for myself, but though it happened over forty years ago I remember my own confirmation as though it happened yesterday, so strong was the presence of the Spirit.

And what could be wrong with any of that, you ask? After all, could there possibly be anything more important for us to teach our children than to keep the commandments?

But do you recognize the contradictory position that question puts you in? Isn't it interesting how what seemed like such an easy answer all of a sudden just got stuck in your throat? After all, isn't there actually something that is much more important for us to teach than just keeping the commandments?

My point here is that we do a magnificent job of teaching our children, and our older members too, the importance of actually doing what Father has commanded them. But I believe that we are far less adept at teaching how to deal with what happens when the inevitable occurs. You know, what happens when we actually break a commandment?

Here is an example of what we're talking about: About twenty years ago, when I was serving as the Young Men president in our stake, we had just finished a Sunday evening youth fireside at the stake center. The meeting had been a presentation by the local police department about the kind of drug problems that were being seen at that point in time. It is my recollection that everyone involved, even during a question-and-answer session after the main message was completed, had handled the meeting very appropriately.

During the question-and-answer period, a man who appeared to be in his mid-twenties raised his hand and said a few things to the young people about the effects that drugs and alcohol had on his life when he was a little younger. To me, his comments had appeared honest and heartfelt. I remember thinking what a great thing it is to know of the reality of the Atonement and the opportunity that it provides us to deal with the negative effects of our poor choices. I had been grateful for his willingness to share his very personal feelings with our young people.

In a brief conversation just after the meeting ended, one of the priesthood leaders in the stake said something along the line of, "That guy seemed to be saying, 'Look at me with my gold chains and open-collared shirt. Look at me with my long blond hair and my problem-filled past. Just look at everything I've done, and all I had to do was repent a little and now everything is fine.' " He then continued something along this line: "If we teach our kids that all they have to do when they make a mistake is go talk to the bishop and repent, they will think that forgiveness is easy and that it's okay to break any commandment they want to."

I was shocked at the response, but only a little less so than I have been at some other responses I have heard when serious mistakes have been made. Compare my priesthood leader's sentiments to these and see if you don't find some commonality.

"I would rather bury you than ever have you be immoral." (Note the actual quotation marks. I heard this one myself as one of my parents attempted to explain the importance of moral purity. I was thirteen at the time.) Or how about this one: "I would rather have you come home in a box than with a dishonorable discharge from your mission." Maybe this one will ring a bell: "You would be better off dead than living the gay lifestyle." Here's a painful one: "If you get pregnant before marriage you will be forced to leave our home and have the baby somewhere else." And last of all: "After everything you have done to hurt us and destroy yourself, you are dead to us. You are no longer a part of our family. You are no longer welcome here, and we never want to see you again."

Isn't it interesting that all these comments have been made by active church members? Those who understand the gospel and are doing things the way they should by attending their meetings, paying a full tithing, holding regular family home evenings, serving in a calling, studying the scriptures, and attending the temple on a regular basis.

You know, they are the ones keeping the commandments. Or at least they think they are.

It is as though we have convinced ourselves that there is only one way to hold to the iron rod. Now there's an interesting thought. Is there really more than one way to hold to the iron rod, or must we all walk on the right side of the rod and hold on with our left hand? Or maybe you would rather we all walk on the left side and hang on with our right hand? How about going hand over hand just to make sure we don't let go even for the briefest of seconds? Does it make any difference if we walk at arm's length from the rod, or must we always have our torso rubbing against it too?

Maybe just hanging onto the rod isn't enough. Maybe we need to try walking on top of the rod like it was a balance beam or a tight rope. And if you want to make it really challenging, how about trying to ride a bike down the rod? It would speed the process and prove to Father how totally serious we are about being right on top of things.

Ludicrous, you say? But are these ideas any more ludicrous than the comments just mentioned? I think not.

Of all the things I will never understand in mortality—of all the things

I never want to understand—nothing will ever be more incomprehensible to me than how someone who claims to be a follower of Jesus Christ could ever say any of these things to or about anyone, let alone to a family member. What about the twenty-second chapter of Matthew, where Christ himself said, "Thou shalt love the Lord thy God with all thy heart, and with all thy soul, and with all thy mind. This is the first and great commandment. And the second is like unto it, Thou shalt love thy neighbor as thyself. On these two commandments hang *all* the law and the prophets" (Matthew 22:37–40; italics added).

Why such things happen

There are many who would say that statements such as these are last-ditch efforts to convince wayward children of the error of their ways. Others would claim that their comments are the verbal equivalent of the tough love my wife and I exhibited when we returned our child to the camper in the middle of winter. Still others are simply convinced of the correctness of their feelings and opinions. And finally there are those who—even after everything they have read thus far—would still try to say, "But, Alan, you don't understand how much it hurts."

For me there can only be one response to those who would ever say such things. It is simply that they do not understand the real meaning of the fall of Adam and the fact that "all have sinned, and come short of the glory of God" (Romans 3:23). They do not understand the real meaning of the statement "I the Lord cannot look upon sin with the *least* degree of allowance" (D&C 1:31; italics added). Further, to make such a statement requires someone to either be so convinced of their personal righteousness as to conveniently ignore the reality of their own lost and fallen state, or to be under the delusion that the severity of one sin compared to another actually makes a difference as to whether they can inherit the celestial kingdom or not. Such is obviously not the case.

So in the two scriptures above, *all* means everyone, no exceptions; and *least degree* means that there is no wiggle room, not for any of us! So it doesn't matter what your child, spouse, or parent has done to you; it doesn't matter how terribly they have treated you; it doesn't matter how badly they have broken your heart; it doesn't even matter if they have actually killed someone. You are in your own boat right there next to theirs, bailing away at the ocean of your own sins in a futile attempt to keep from sinking into the oblivion of darkness that justice demands of us all. And there you will stay until you turn to the Savior with full purpose of heart and allow him to heal the damage that you have done to the boat that is your life, for he is the only one who knows both how and where to make the needed repairs.

It would also seem appropriate to make a comparison between this kind of thinking and that involved with the woman who was taken in adultery. The story is a familiar one, but three points bear repeating. First is the fact that the woman was taken in the very act and there was no question as to her guilt or innocence. Second is the fact that adultery carried a death sentence at that time, so those who found her in the act had every legal right to carry out such a sentence. Third is the fact that the judge she was taken before—Christ himself—is the creator of the universe and the only one who actually had the right to, and ultimately will, pass judgment upon her.

Surely you remember the Savior's comment to the scribes and Pharisees, those who kept the commandments, at least in their own minds. He said, "He that is without sin among you, let him first cast a stone at her" (John 8:7). Then after those supposedly righteous men—being so pointedly reminded of their own lost and fallen state—quickly left, he whose literal right it was to condemn this woman to an eternity of misery and woe simply said, "Neither do I condemn thee: go, and sin no more" (John 8:11).

And here are the hardest questions of them all. When parents make statements such as these, when the attitudes and understandings that are addressed throughout this entire book are displayed, is it because we honestly believe it is our right to pass such judgment and that we are justified in doing so, or is it simply that we lack the faith and perspective that is required to let all things happen in good time and in God's time?

Do we make such statements with the understanding that by doing so we are in fact placing ourselves ahead of both God and Christ in our ability to know the heart and mind of our child? Do we so easily forget the temple covenants that we made with our spouse? Do we forget the Savior's command that "what therefore God hath joined together, let not man put asunder" (Matthew 19:6).

Do we have so little understanding of the order of heaven that we lose sight of the fact that it is only Christ who is "mighty to save" (2 Nephi 31:19)?

Have we forgotten, or is it that we simply choose to ignore, Father's statement that "he that forgiveth not his brother [or his child] his trespasses standeth condemned before the Lord; *for there remaineth in him the greater sin*. I, the Lord, will forgive whom I will forgive, but of you it is required to forgive *all* men" (D&C 64:9–10; italics added)?

Or is it simply that our own perspective is so narrow and our understanding so limited that we have convinced ourselves that the sins are so many and so serious that it is no longer possible for our child—or maybe it's you and me—to repent and be made whole and clean once more?

All of this can only lead to one conclusion, and that is simply that we do not understand the relationship between grace, faith, works, and the power of the infinite Atonement to heal and change our lives.

6.2 Obedience vs. Understanding

OF ALL THE STATEMENTS OF TRUTH THAT HAVE COME from the treatment program that we are involved in, none has been more profound to me than this one: "Religion is for those who don't want to go to hell. Spirituality is for those who have been to hell and don't want to go back." There are several different tracks that could be followed from such a saying, but since practical application is far more important than academic accuracy, you are just going to have to put up with my explanation of its meaning.

Because of the youth of the people involved and given the seriousness of their situations, it seems to me that this statement is intended to make a distinction between the religion of their parents—what to our children appears to be a life of thoughtless routines and mechanical repetition, or more simply, keeping the commandments—and the absolute necessity of them developing their own relationship with God. Further, because everything in the treatment program is non-denominational and based on the twelve-step program of Alcoholics Anonymous, that relationship is specifically defined as being with God, as they understand him. It sounds to me like Bill W.—the man who wrote the twelve steps, founded AA, and is the patron saint of alcoholics and addicts the world over— was trying to get us to meet people wherever they are in their ability to relate to God, which, given the thinking problems that addiction creates in the first place, makes a whole lot of sense to me.

And with those thoughts as a foundation, this discussion could go off into some really interesting directions. But let's see if the following story can keep us focused on practical application rather than on the need to either teach correct principles or to simply keep the commandments.

Because of the tremendous challenges that she faced and overcame, Helen Keller lived one of the most inspirational lives that we know of. At nineteen months of age she was stricken both blind and deaf by a still undiagnosed illness—it was probably either scarlet fever or meningitis—and her life and her parents' lives were forever changed. The following years proved very hard for Helen and her family as she became a very difficult child, smashing dishes and lamps and terrorizing the whole household with her screaming and temper tantrums. Relatives regarded her as a monster and thought she should be put into an institution.

Finally Helen's mother learned of the Perkins Institution and Massachusetts Asylum for the Blind. After a consultation with its director, it was recommended that Annie Sullivan become Helen's teacher, and so began a most remarkable teacher-student relationship. Annie moved to Alabama and immediately began trying to teach Helen by finger-spelling words into her hand. First she spelled *doll*, then *cake*, and so on. Helen was curious and loved having words spelled into her hand, but was unable to make the connection between the finger movements in her hand and the object that was associated with those movements. Her behavior continued to be a major source of contention and problems, but now those problems were not just between Helen and her parents; they were also between Annie and the Kellers as they all tried to determine the best way to help Helen.

After about two weeks of working with the family and trying to make the needed breakthrough, Annie realized she would need to isolate Helen from her family to break the behavior cycles that had become so ingrained in all of them. So she bargained with the Kellers to allow her to take Helen to a small cottage where they could be alone, for only in that environment would Helen be forced to deal with Annie and her more appropriate rules of behavior, rather than the indulgence and enabling that had become the family norm. Does any of that sound familiar from your home?

The first two weeks in the cottage came and went with a marked improvement in Helen's behavior, to the point that for the first time she was able to eat dinner at the family table without spoiling the experience for everyone else. Helen's parents were thrilled at the progress she had made in such a short time, but Annie knew that the real breakthrough still had not come. She knew that while Helen was more obedient and pleasant than before, what was happening had to do with obedience only, and that there was no real understanding behind the behavior.

Helen's parents were so overjoyed with her progress that when Annie suggested that she be allowed to remain at the cottage until the needed awakening came, they steadfastly refused. Their logic was that since so much progress had been made, and because they missed her so terribly, it was cruel and unnatural to keep her from their association.

In the play written about this time in her life, Helen's father compliments Annie on what she has accomplished in such a short time. Annie's responses are some of the greatest stage quotes of all time. She says, "I taught her one thing, no. Don't do this, don't do that . . . I wanted to teach her what language is. I wanted to teach her yes."

Captain Keller responds, "You will have time.

To which Annie says, "I don't know how. I know without it to do nothing but obey is—no gift, *obedience without understanding is a—blindness, too.* Is that all I've wished on her? . . . Maybe. I don't know what else to do. Simply go on, keep doing what I've done, and have—faith that inside she's—That inside it's waiting. Like water, underground. All I can do is keep on."[1]

So it is with all of us and our precious children. For if all we ever hear is, "Keep the commandments"—which we interpret as, "You must be perfect, and you can never make a mistake"—without help understanding the reasons why, then when the inevitable mistakes happen and when the even more inevitable withdrawal of the Spirit follows, we are all bewildered by the loss of that Spirit and left with the uncertainty, doubt, and outright fear that are a natural by-product of the gathering darkness.

So if we do not continuously teach of the grace of God through the Atonement of Jesus Christ, if we do not plainly and constantly teach that there is a way for all of us to repair the damage that has been done, if we are obedient but without any real understanding of our place in the grand plan of salvation, is it any wonder that there are so many who misinterpret the partial withdrawal of the Spirit as an utter and complete condemnation?

And if we do not understand the reality of the love of God and Christ, how can there be any wonder that so many succumb to the adversary's screaming of their complete worthlessness and utter failure?

Further, if we do not teach of the simplicity of the path, if all we teach is the temporal law of performances and ordinances, how can we expect anyone, but especially our children, to "get it" any more quickly than the forty years that it took the children of Israel while they wandered in the desert?

And here is something I found through a coworker. Once again, it comes from the world of Alcoholics Anonymous, and I think it's a wonderful way to finish our discussion about what we teach and our attitudes about parenting.

"Letting Go"

To let go does not mean to stop caring; it means I can't do it for someone else.

To let go is not to cut myself off; it's the realization that I can't do it for another.

To let go is not to enable, but to allow learning from natural consequences.

To let go means to admit powerlessness, which means the outcome is not in my hands.

To let go is not to change or blame another; it's to make the most out of myself.

To let go is not to care for, but to care about.

To let go is not to fix, but to be supportive.

To let go is not to judge, but to allow another to be a human being.

To let go is not to be in the middle of arranging all the outcomes, but to allow others to affect their destinies.

To let go is not to be protective; it's to permit another to face reality.

To let go is not to deny, but to accept.

To let go is not to nag, scold, or argue; but instead to search out our own shortcomings and correct them.

To let go is not to adjust everything to my desires, but to take each day as it comes and cherish myself in it.

To let go is not to criticize and regulate anybody, but to try to become what I dream I can be.

To let go is not to regret the past, but to grow and live for the future.

To let go is to fear less and LOVE MORE.

—Author Unknown

Notes

1. William Gibson, *The Miracle Worker*, act 3, 1960; italics added.

6.3 Grace, Faith, and Works—The Chicken or the Egg?

IT SHOULD BE PLAINLY OBVIOUS THAT THERE IS NOT SPACE enough left in these pages to even begin to address the intricacies of the relationship between these three doctrines—grace, faith, and works. However, there are a few comments from another source that seem appropriate.

Brother Stephen E. Robinson has written a wonderful book called *Believing Christ.* In that book he makes the following comments,

> For centuries theologians have argued pointlessly over whether individuals are save by faith or saved by works. A pox on both their houses, for neither by faith alone (defining faith as mere passive belief) nor by works alone are we saved. Salvation comes through a covenant relationship in which both faith and works play their parts. To insist that salvation comes by works alone, that we can earn it ourselves without needing the grace of God, insults the mercy of God and mocks the sacrifice of Jesus Christ in our behalf. On the other hand, to insist that salvation comes by belief alone and that God places no other obligations upon the believer insults the justice of God and makes Christ the minister of sin.[1]

And with those thoughts in mind, consider the following scriptures:

> Therefore, cheer up your hearts, and remember that ye are free to act for yourselves—to choose the way of everlasting death or the way of eternal life. Wherefore, my beloved brethren, reconcile yourselves to the will of God, and not to the will of the devil and the flesh; and remember, *after* ye are reconciled unto God, that it is *only* in and through

> the grace of God that ye are saved. Wherefore, may God raise you from death by the power of the resurrection, and also from everlasting death by the power of the atonement, that ye may be received into the eternal kingdom of God, that ye may praise him through grace divine. Amen. (2 Nephi 10:23–25; italics added)

And then,

> For we labor diligently to write, to persuade our children, and also our brethren, to believe in Christ, and to be reconciled to God; for we know that it is by grace that we are saved, after all we can do. . . . and we are made alive in Christ because of our faith; . . . And we talk of Christ, we rejoice in Christ, we preach of Christ, we prophesy of Christ, and we write according to our prophecies, that our children may know to what source they may look for a remission of their sins. (2 Nephi 25:23–26)

And finally,

> Yea, come unto Christ, and be perfected in him, and deny yourselves of all ungodliness; and if ye shall deny yourselves of all ungodliness, and love God with all your might, mind and strength, then is his grace sufficient for you, that by his grace ye may be perfect in Christ; and if by the grace of God ye are perfect in Christ, ye can in nowise deny the power of God. And again, if ye by the grace of God are perfect in Christ, and deny not his power, then are ye sanctified in Christ by the grace of God, through the shedding of the blood of Christ, which is in the covenant of the Father unto the remission of your sins, that ye become holy, without spot. (Moroni 10:32–33)

So, after everything we can do for ourselves, even if we were to develop our self-awareness to the point that we were actually choosing to keep every commandment that Father has ever given, we would still be lost and would fall a very long way short of the absolute perfection that is required to be able to return to live in his presence again.

This is frustrating and depressing enough for an adult. But if we who are older and have more life experience can struggle so mightily with these concepts, how can we be surprised at the difficulty our young people have with them too? After all, just remember how long it has taken you to reach your current level of understanding and spiritual maturity.

And here is another of those really tough questions, but it's tough for a different reason from those posed a little earlier. What approach do we use, what do we need to understand—specifically—so that we can teach everyone, but especially our children, to help them understand and begin applying the healing power of the Atonement of Jesus Christ to their own lives? It seems to me that the scriptures have three different examples that are very straightforward and easy to understand.

Story number one begins in the Old Testament during the time when the children of Israel were wandering in the wilderness. It begins,

> And the people spake against God, and against Moses. . . . And the Lord sent fiery serpents among the people, and they bit the people; and much people of Israel died. Therefore the people came to Moses, and said, We have sinned, for we have spoken against the Lord, and against thee; pray unto the Lord, that he take away the serpents from us. And Moses prayed for the people. And the Lord said unto Moses, Make thee a fiery serpent, and set it upon a pole: and it shall come to pass, that every one that is bitten, when he looketh upon it, shall live. And Moses made a serpent of brass, and put it upon a pole, and it came to pass, that if a serpent had bitten any man, when he beheld the serpent of brass, he lived. (Numbers 21:5–9)

So the children of Israel murmured against both Father and his prophet—again. Not a wise choice on their part. But they were just like our children, young and inexperienced in the workings of the Spirit. In this case, Father was a little more direct in his attempt to get their attention than he usually is, so the poisonous serpents came and started biting people, which led to a significant number of deaths. Not surprisingly, they started paying a little more attention to their relationship with God and decided to ask Moses for help too. Imagine their reaction to his solution to the problem. After all, the snakes were all around them and people were dying from their bites. Moses gave what to some had to be a ridiculous solution. He told them that all they had to do to be saved from the danger was simply turn and look at the brazen serpent that he had raised on a pole.

How would you react to such a situation? Would that solution seem so easy as to be laughable? Would you have looked at Moses and told him to get real, you know, come up with something a little more rational? You wouldn't have been alone if you had, any more so than you are now if you are more interested in emphasizing keeping the commandments over knowing and loving God through his Son, Jesus Christ.

Consider the commentary from the book of Alma regarding the reaction of the children of Israel:

> Thou art angry, O Lord, with this people, because they will not understand thy mercies which thou hast bestowed upon them because of thy Son. . . . behold . . . the Son of God . . . was spoken of by Moses; yea, and behold a type was raised up in the wilderness, that whosoever would look upon it might live. And many did look and live. But few understood the meaning of those things, and this because of the hardness of their hearts. But there were many who were so hardened that they would not look, therefore they perished. Now the reason they would not look is because they did not believe that it would heal them. O my brethren, if ye could be healed by merely casting about your eyes that ye might be healed, would ye not behold quickly, or would ye rather harden your hearts in unbelief, and be slothful, that ye would not cast about your eyes, that ye might perish? If so, wo shall come upon you; but if not so, then cast about your eyes and begin to believe in the Son of God. (Alma 33:16–22)

So Alma tells us that a prophet named Zenock understood the specific causes of the Children of Israel's unwillingness to "look to God and live" (Alma 37:47). Isn't it interesting that the first thing he comments on is their lack of understanding of Father's mercies, of his desire that we all recognize the simplicity of the process of getting on the path that leads back to him? And isn't it just a little frightening that the major cause of that lack of understanding was that they had hardened their hearts to the easiness of the way? And does that description hit just a little too close to home for your comfort?

Then comes a much better known and more often talked about incident from the life of the Savior, that of the woman who touched the hem of his garment. It reads,

> And a woman having an issue of blood twelve years, which had spent all her living upon physicians, neither could be healed of any, Came behind him, and touched the border of his garment: and immediately her issue of blood stanched. And Jesus said, Who touched me? When all denied, Peter and they that were with him said, Master, the multitude throng thee and press thee, and sayest thou, Who touched me? And Jesus said, Somebody hath touched me: for I perceive that virtue is gone out of me. And when the woman saw that she was not hid, she came trembling, and falling down before him, she declared unto him before all the people for what cause she had touched him, and how she was healed immediately. And he said unto her, Daughter, be of good comfort: thy faith hath made thee whole: go in peace. (Luke 8:43–48)

This example is interesting because it is probably a little better representation of the actual effort that is required of each of us. In this case the woman had to at least put forth the effort to be on the street where Jesus would be passing by, but the concept that simply reaching out and touching the hem of his cloak would be enough to heal her was strictly her own idea.

So the question is, What part of your life is "having an issue of blood" and in need of repair, and do you have the simple faith that it takes to position yourself so as to be able to reach out and touch the border of his garment?

Or does that make the process easier than you think it should be, or than you want it to be?

Then consider the example of Alma the Younger and his experience with the process. It reads,

> For when I heard the words—If thou wilt be destroyed of thyself, seek no more to destroy the church of God—I was struck with such great fear and amazement lest perhaps I should be destroyed, that I fell to the earth. . . . And now, for three days and for three nights was I racked, even with the pains of a damned soul. And it came to pass that as I was thus racked with torment, while I was harrowed up by the memory of my many sins, behold, I remembered also to have heard my father prophesy unto the people concerning the coming of one Jesus Christ, a Son of God, to atone for the sins of the world. Now, as my mind caught hold upon this thought, I cried within my heart: O Jesus, thou Son of God, have mercy on me, who am in the gall of bitterness, and am encircled about by the everlasting chains of death. And now, behold, when I thought this, I could remember my pains no more: yea, I was harrowed up by the memory of my sins no more. And oh, what joy, and what marvelous light I did behold; yea, my soul was fill with joy as exceeding as was my pain! (Alma 36:11–20)

Therefore, Alma's experience with the angel got him to the point that he actually understood his lost and fallen state before God, which properly focused his mind on the need for him to change his life and move in a different direction. But pay special attention to how quickly his relief came. Note his specific comment that it was "when I thought this"—when he simply processed the thought asking Jesus Christ to have mercy on him—"I could remember my pains no more: yea, I was harrowed up by the memory of my sins no more."

And are you screaming, "But, Alan, it's not that easy! It takes at least months, if not years, to be forgiven of our sins!"?

To which I respond: Yes, it can take that long. But only for those who know and understand the law before they transgress against it. For only those who know the law—only those who know Christ—are accountable to that law. "For behold that all little children are alive in Christ, *and also all they that are without the law. For the power of redemption cometh on all them that have no law; wherefore, he that is not condemned, or he that is under no condemnation, cannot repent*" (Moroni 8:22; italics added).

We must also make a distinction between the amount of time it takes for Father to forgive us of our sins—and us to forgive ourselves too—and the amount of time that it takes for us to deal with the effects of our sins. That is an entirely different matter because now we are back to talking about how and what we allow ourselves to think, and the impact that that thinking has on our feelings, emotions, and behavior. I truly hope there is an increased understanding of those concepts after your reading of Principles Three and Four, and I also hope you realize that what is contained here can only be a starting point for you to begin expanding your understanding of these very critical subjects.

And yes, I also understand that this scripture is specifically talking about those who are younger than eight years of age, and also about those who do not have the mental capacity to learn and reason beyond an eight-year-old's level. However, we also need to ask the question, Is there any difference in Father's judgment between someone who cannot learn and someone who has not yet learned? For isn't someone who does not yet know Christ simply in the same position that Helen Keller was just before she made the connection between the finger movements in her one hand and the water running through the fingers of her other?

And doesn't that distinction make all the difference?

After all, how many examples are there of people who have done everything "right"—you know, gone to church meetings and activities regularly, graduated from Seminary, gone on a mission, and been married in the temple—only to fall by the wayside later on as the trials and temptations of adulthood come their way? And how many examples are there of those who have made some pretty serious mistakes in their youth and then been able to set things right with Father and move on to a productive adult life filled with family activities and church involvement? I personally know of more than a few in both categories.

This just reinforces the critical difference between external appearances and the sometimes very different internal reality that we all live with but don't like to acknowledge. So we are once again confronted with the need to determine who knows what—and when they know it—in order to make a righteous determination of their guilt or innocence before the law. Or maybe it would just be easier to "forgive all men" (D&C 64:10), as Father has commanded us to, and leave the judgment to those who have either the right or the responsibility to do so. You know, either the God of Heaven or those who are his chosen servants within the priesthood line of authority.

I can hear it now: "But, Alan, you don't understand. These people, these children, have been taught better. They have been taught the principles of the gospel and of the importance of following Christ in their lives. They know better!" Yes, they do. And so did Alma the Younger! But it was not until he understood his lost and fallen state before God in his own heart, mind, and spirit that he became answerable to the fullness of the law. He was racked with guilt and torment because of his actions due to the presence of the Light of Christ, which is "in all and through all things, the light of truth" (D&C 88:6). This is the same Spirit that warns us of the danger of our actions before we are fully accountable before the law, and it is the withdrawal of this Spirit that causes so many problems for us and our children, as described in the chapters of Principle Four.

So what is the answer to this question of grace, faith, and works? Which of these comes first, and which leads to the other? Which is the chicken and which is the egg? To answer that question, we need to turn to 2 Nephi 31:13, for that is the place where we find the best summation of the process in all of the entirety of the scriptures. Nephi says, "I know that if ye shall follow the Son, with full purpose of heart, acting no hypocrisy and no deception before God, but with real intent, repenting of your sins, . . . then cometh the baptism of fire and of the Holy Ghost; and then can ye speak with the tongue of angels, and shout praises unto the Holy One of Israel."

He continues,

> And now, my beloved brethren, after ye have gotten into this strait and narrow path, I would ask if all is done? Behold, I say unto you Nay; for ye have not come thus far save it were by the word of Christ with unshaken faith in him, relying wholly upon the merits of him who is might to save. Wherefore, *ye must press forward with a steadfastness in*

> *Christ, having a perfect brightness of hope, and a love of God and of all men.* Wherefore, if ye shall press forward, feasting upon the word of Christ, and endure to the end, behold, thus saith the Father: Ye shall have eternal life. And now, behold, my beloved brethren, this is the way; and there is none other way nor name given under heaven whereby man can be saved in the kingdom of God. And now, behold, this is the doctrine of Christ, and the only and true doctrine of the Father, and of the Son, and of the Holy Ghost. (2 Nephi 31:19–21; italics added)

All of this can only lead to the conclusion that Jesus Christ is "Alpha and Omega, the beginning and the ending" (Revelation 1:8). He is both the chicken and the egg, if you will. And until we understand that fact—that it is only in and through him and his sacrifice on our behalf that we can even think of returning to Father's presence—we are lost and fallen and "of all men most miserable" (1 Corinthians 15:19).

Notes

1. Stephen E. Robinson, *Believing Christ* (Salt Lake City: Bookcraft, 2002), 69–70.

6.4 "Lord, How Is It Done?"

THE QUOTE THAT TITLES THIS CHAPTER COMES FROM YET another example of Father's goodness to one of his children. In Enos's case, it took him a day and a night of constant prayer to get his mind and heart to the point that Father was willing to say, "Thy sins are forgiven thee" (Enos 1:5). But it is very interesting that he says his desire to do so came because "the words which I had often heard my father speak concerning eternal life, and the joy of the saints, sunk deep into my heart" (Enos 1:3).

So, Enos's father regularly taught him of the joy that living the gospel brings, and that concept—the gospel as a good and happy thing rather than a daily drudgery to keep the commandments and strive in vain to be perfect—motivated Enos to spend some time on his knees and find out about the reality of God for himself.

There's a good chance that we can learn something from that approach.

I hope there's a chance that framing the comment that way makes more sense now than it would have before you read the chapters of Principle Three. Because, as with virtually everything we ever try to teach or learn, the approach that we use is critical to the clarity with which the message is received. Here is another analogy of the process that might prove useful.

As new kids come into the treatment program that we are now involved in, they get to do what is called an intro. That means that during the weekly open meeting—the only time when all the kids and their families are in the same room at the same time—the child will stand in front of the entire group and face their family. Given the fluctuation in head count at any given time, that means that there are probably between 300 and 350 people in the room when this happens. When kids give their intros, they include the following information:

- Their names and ages
- How many days they have been in treatment and whether they think they need to be there or not
- Their complete drug list, including the drug of choice
- Their complete compulsion list, including the compulsion of choice
- Four past incidents, including one with family, friends, school, and the law
- Any realizations they have made thus far
- Two short-term goals and one long-term goal

An intro usually happens in the first two to three weeks of treatment, and prior to that time the only contact the child has had with their family is to stand and say, "I love you" across the room to each other. Needless to say, there are lots of emotions and tears as parents find out the full extent of the deception that has been going on, and as the kids are forced to confront the reality of the impact that their actions have had on their family.

In the nine months that we have been involved, I would guess that we have listened to almost 120 intros. The drug lists have included everything that you have ever heard of and probably some that you haven't; the compulsion lists run the gamut from lying and manipulating to sexually acting out to self-mutilation and eating disorders to just about anything else you can think of; school incidents once again span the entire spectrum of inappropriate behavior; and thankfully the legal incidents are usually nothing more than problems related to school or fairly minor drug possession charges.

When the child is through with the intro, their family has a chance to respond to what has been said. This is the real reason to go into this much detail about the process. Parents are cautioned to only talk about their feelings and not to lecture their child, and it has been a fascinating experience to watch so many families from so many different backgrounds go through this experience. Only twice have I seen or heard parents who were genuinely angry with their children.

What have we seen? Relief, confusion, guilt, frustration, grief, terror at the drug and compulsion lists, outright fear, and a host of others. And in the same breath virtually every parent has expressed admiration for their child's willingness to stand in front of that kind of group and be that point-blank honest. For most of us it has been the first time in a very long time that we have known for sure that our child was telling us the truth. Big, tough young men have cried like little boys, and their even tougher fathers have sobbed in mute silence because of the love they feel for their child and the utter relief at their safety. These are some of the most tender scenes that I will ever see in my life and I am a far better person because of the experience.

And then there is the love. When relations have been as strained and damaged as those that are involved in this type of program, it comes from somewhere way down deep in the soul. That's because the danger and fear are so real. But after what can only be described as a gut-wrenching experience, when such a broad spectrum of parents just want to tell their children how much they love them, when they want to talk about how relieved they are for their children's safety, when they just want to express pride in their children's honesty and smile with hope for a brighter and more positive future, there must be a lesson for all of us about how we treat others when they make mistakes, especially small ones.

So, regardless of how large or small the problem is, the key to building a real relationships with anyone, but especially a child or spouse, is making the specific choice to express love and appreciation for even the smallest of their positive behaviors.

Why even the smallest successes, you ask? Because if all those close to us hear is admonition and correction, if all they hear is criticism and conflict, if all they get is put-downs and smack-downs, when the time comes that they accomplish something that is important and positive to them and we then give the appropriate positive comments, they will not be able to believe us when we say those good things to them. Those kind of positive and reinforcing words will be so foreign coming from our lips that their impact is actually negated because those we care about most have been conditioned not to expect or believe anything but negativity and criticism coming from us.

6.5 Sober Thinking

THERE MAY BE SOME WHO WILL LOOK AT THE ITEMS that follow and find them trite and over simplified. If you happen to be one of those, just realize that that says more about your current level of understanding than it does about the importance of the things on the list, for these are some of the most powerful concepts that you will ever come across. Also, for the purposes of this discussion, though the term *sober thinking* specifically includes the kind of thinking that helps any of us to avoid drugs or alcohol, in this case it should be expanded to include our thinking about any of the challenges or thought processes that are addressed throughout this book.

The Four Signs of Sober Thinking
Think, think, think
First things first
Easy does it
One day at a time

Five Criteria for Sober Thinking
Based on objective reality
Protects my life and health
Produces goals
Helps me to feel and act the way I need to
Keeps me out of significant conflict with myself and others

You may look at those two lists and think that they don't apply to you unless you or someone close to you is already involved in some kind of problem behavior. But then again, you might read through them and find that they apply more to your life than you thought. After all, who among us couldn't afford to do a little more thinking and a lot less reacting in life? Which of us wouldn't be helped greatly by doing the most important thing first, taking things a whole lot easier, and simply living life one day at a time?

And just how objective is your reality? Do you take the appropriate precautions to protect your life and health, or are there lots of ways you need to work on that one? When was the last time you wrote down a goal and spent any time trying to find different ways to make that goal happen? Do you live your life on your terms, or do you spend your time trying to find out what others want and need to the exclusion of your own dreams, aspirations, and inspirations? And does that approach bring you the joy that Father says you are entitled to, or are you in constant conflict with yourself and others?

Let's consider the AA Serenity Prayer: "God, grant me the serenity to accept the things I cannot change, the courage to change the things I can, and the wisdom to know the difference." Have you ever analyzed the power of these few words and considered the impact that following this simple prayer could have on your life? If not, read it again and see if there isn't something here that might help you in your life.

And how about the twelve steps? Do you believe that because the steps weren't developed under Church auspices they can't be inspired? I'll grant you that unless you either are an addict yourself, or you have a child or loved one who is, it's unlikely that you have ever even read them. But there are few blueprints for improving you life that are more powerful.

1. We admitted we were powerless over our addiction and that our lives had become unmanageable.
2. Came to believe that a Power greater than ourselves could restore us to sanity.
3. Made a decision to turn our will and our life over to the care of God, as we understood him.
4. Made a searching and fearless moral inventory of ourselves.
5. Admitted to God, to ourselves and to another human being, the exact nature of our wrongs.

6. Were entirely ready to have God remove these defects of character.
7. Humbly asked Him to remove our shortcomings.
8. Made a list of all persons we had harmed, and became willing to make amends to them all.
9. Made direct amends to such people wherever possible, except when to do so would injure them or others.
10. Continued to take personal inventory, and when we were wrong promptly admitted it.
11. Sought through prayer and meditation to improve our conscious contact with God, as we understood Him, praying only for knowledge of His will for us and the power to carry that out.
12. Having had a spiritual awakening as the result of these steps, we tried to carry this message to others, and to practice these principles in all our affairs.

These steps are so powerful and all encompassing that the leaders of our Church have adopted them as the template for their efforts to help those dealing with addictions in all their varieties. All that has been added is scriptural support for each of the steps. Why have they taken this approach? Because these steps have been proven to be the most powerful and successful program in the entire world at helping people to deal with the problems that addiction has created in their lives. But as has been described throughout this entire book, because the thinking processes involved in any addiction, sin, or disorder are the same, the solutions to all of those are also the same.

So it doesn't matter if the inspiration comes directly from the scriptures, or if its beginnings come from the twelve steps. Father is still the God of Heaven, and he is always willing to reach out to us whenever we reach out to him.

6.6 The Importance of Maintaining an Eternal Perspective

OF ALL THE DIFFERENT PSYCHOLOGICAL TOOLS THAT MY wife and I have used, of all the different thinking and attitude concepts that we have read, of everything that we have been exposed to over the last nine years, nothing has provided more comfort and given us more relief from the stress and pain of our lives than the sure knowledge that Father is in control and that all is playing out exactly as he knew it would.

Chief among the pillars that we have leaned on is a talk given back in 1992 by President Boyd K. Packer. It is entitled "Our Moral Environment." I recommend it highly for anyone dealing with challenges or anyone close to someone who is struggling, not just parents.

> The measure of our success as parents, however, will not rest solely on how our children turn out. That judgment would be just *only if we could raise our families in a perfectly moral environment*, and that now is not possible. It is not uncommon for responsible parents to lose one of their children, for a time, to influences over which they have no control. They agonize over rebellious sons or daughters. They are puzzled over why they are so helpless when they have tried so hard to do what they should. It is my conviction that those wicked influences one day will be overruled.[1]

So we are once again forced to confront the difficulty of the task that lies before us all. And if the task was that difficult fifteen years ago—do we even remember a time when the Internet was not an omnipresent part of our world?—how much more difficult has it become in the intervening years?

But these words from President Packer are intended to do far more than acknowledge the difficulty of being a parent in today's world, for he is also telling us that when the time of final judgment arrives, all things will be taken into account by a God who is not only just, but merciful too. And as a further clarification of this idea please refer to D&C 46:15, which reads, "And again, to some it is given by the Holy Ghost to know the differences of administration, as it will be pleasing unto the same Lord, according as the Lord will, suiting his mercies according to the conditions of the children of men."

Elder Packer then uses two quotes from early Church leaders to further explain his position. As you read them now, see if they don't provide a little different perspective on the critical importance of the sealing covenant and the true meaning of being an eternal family.

> "The Prophet Joseph Smith declared—and he never taught a more comforting doctrine—that the eternal sealings of faithful parents and the divine promises made to them for valiant service in the Cause of Truth, would save not only themselves, but likewise their posterity. Though some of the sheep may wander, the eye of the Shepherd is upon them, and sooner or later they will feel the tentacles of Divine Providence reaching out after them and drawing them back to the fold. Either in this life or the life to come, they will return. They will have to pay their debt to justice; they will suffer for their sins; and may tread a thorny path; but if it leads them at last, like the penitent Prodigal, to a loving and forgiving father's heart and home, the painful experience will not have been in vain. Pray for your careless and disobedient children; hold on to them with your faith. Hope on, trust on, till you see the salvation of God" (Orson F. Whitney, in Conference Report, Apr. 1929, p. 110).
>
> We cannot overemphasize the value of temple marriage, the binding ties of the sealing ordinance, and the standards of worthiness required of them. When parents keep the covenants they have made at the altar of the temple, *their children will be forever bound to them*. President Brigham Young said: "Let the father and mother, who are members of this Church and Kingdom, take a righteous course, and strive with all their might never to do a wrong, but to do good all their lives; if they have one child or one hundred children, if they conduct themselves towards them as they should, binding them to the Lord by their faith and prayers, I care not where those children go, they are bound up to their parents by an everlasting tie, and no power of earth or hell can separate them from their parents in eternity; they will return again to the fountain from whence they sprang" (Joseph Fielding Smith, *Doctrines of Salvation,* comp. Bruce R. McConkie, 3 vols., 2:90–91).[2]

From these quotes we can only conclude that though our children may struggle mightily because of the evil influences that are so prevalent in today's world, even though they may have to "tread a thorny path . . . to pay their debt to justice, the painful experience will not have been in vain, [and] when parents keep the covenants they have made at the altar of the temple [their children] are bound up to their parents by an everlasting tie, and no power of earth or hell can separate them from their parents in eternity" (compiled from the three paragraphs above).

Did you also notice what was said about the importance of the sealing covenant and the absolute necessity of our faithfulness to it? As you read those three paragraphs, do you now understand the fact that while you may not be able to control your children's decision making or behavior here in mortality, what you do in *your* life and the way you interact with your spouse will have a *direct* impact on your children's ability to lay claim on the blessings of the Atonement and the ordinances of the temple?

And praise be to God for the light and knowledge that he showers down upon us through his chosen servants, and for the more eternal perspective that they give us. There are not words enough in the dictionary or space enough in this or any other book to express the gratitude that I feel to a God such as ours, and for the peace that comes to my troubled soul through such inspired leaders and teachers.

"Be still and know that I am God" (Psalm 46:10).

Yes, it's the same quote, but with a different reference. In this case, the psalmist is telling us that, regardless of the difficulty, Father will always be there to comfort us. It reads,

> God is our refuge and strength, a very present help in trouble. Therefore will not we fear, though the earth be removed, and though the mountains be carried into the midst of the sea; Though the waters thereof roar and be troubled, though the mountains shake with the swelling thereof. . . . The heathen raged, the kingdoms were moved: he uttered his voice, the earth melted. The Lord of hosts is with us; the God of Jacob is our refuge. . . . Come behold the works of the Lord, what desolation he hath made in the earth. He maketh wars to cease unto the end of the earth; he breaketh the bow, and cutteth the spear in sunder; he burneth the chariot in the fire. Be still and know that I am God. (Psalm 46:1–10)

From there we are referred to Job 37:14, which can only be described as glorious counsel. It reads, "Hearken unto this, O Job: stand still, and consider the wondrous works of God." So when things get tough, when we are in fear for our children, when the mountains of our lives shake, when the heathen rages and kingdoms are moved, "the God of Jacob is our refuge . . . he maketh wars to cease," and we are told to "be still" and "consider the wondrous works of God."

Is that easy to do? Obviously not. But by putting forth a little more effort to develop our own understanding—there's that word again—maybe, just maybe, we can get to the point that we can continue on, regardless of the difficulty of the challenges.

What follows now are examples of those who have been able to develop that understanding, and these are concepts that have provided even more comfort than those offered by Elder Whitney and Presidents Packer and Young. In fact, these are the greatest comforts that I know of. I hope they can bring the same peace to you that they have brought to me.

Alma the Younger

First we turn to the life of Alma the Younger and part of a sermon that he gave to the people of Gideon. Alma has come to Gideon after reestablishing the Church in Zarahemla, and he immediately begins to teach the people about Jesus Christ and his infinite Atonement. He says,

> And behold, he shall be born of Mary, at Jerusalem. . . . And he shall go forth, suffering pains and afflictions and temptations of every kind; and this that the word might be fulfilled which saith he will take upon him the pains and the sicknesses of his people. And he will take upon him death, that he may loose the bands of death which bind his people; and he will take upon him their infirmities, that his bowels may be filled with mercy, according to the flesh, that he may know according to the flesh how to succor his people according to their infirmities. Now the Spirit knoweth all things; nevertheless the Son of God suffereth according to the flesh that he might take upon him the sins of his people, that he might blot our their transgressions according to the power of his deliverance. (Alma 7:10–13)

Here Alma teaches us that the Savior not only paid the price that justice demands for all of our sins, but that he has also "take[n] upon him the pains and the sicknesses of his people . . . [and] their infirmities." So when we are sick in any fashion, the pain and discomfort associated with that illness—notice that it does not specify any difference between physical and mental illness—is also something that Christ has experienced, and thus he understands how to "succor his people according to their infirmities."

Isaiah

Then we turn to the words of Isaiah, for as Nephi observed, "Great are the words of Isaiah" (3 Nephi 23:1). In Isaiah 53 we read the following:

> He is despised and rejected of men; a man of sorrows, and acquainted with grief: and we hid as it were our faces from him; he was despised, and we esteemed him not. Surely he hath borne our griefs, and carried our sorrows: yet we did esteem him stricken, smitten of God, and afflicted. But he was wounded for our transgressions, he was bruised for our iniquities: the chastisement of our peace was upon him; and with his stripes we are healed. All we like sheep have gone astray; we have turned every one to his own way; and the Lord hath laid on him the iniquity of us all. He was oppressed, and he was afflicted, yet he opened not his mouth; he is brought as a lamb to the slaughter, and as a sheep before her shearers is dumb, so he openeth not his mouth. (Isaiah 53:3–7)

Thus the bar that is his suffering is raised ever higher. For he was despised, wounded, bruised, chastised, and beaten. He has borne grief, sorrow, iniquity, oppression, and affliction, and yet he "openeth not his mouth."

Once again, praise be to God! For were it not so, the Atonement could not accurately be called infinite because it could not have infinite application and it would not be able to cover every pain, affliction, temptation, infirmity, grief, sorrow, iniquity, oppression, affliction, and sin.

Joseph Smith

On October 27, 1838, Governor Lilburn W. Boggs of Missouri issued a general extermination order, which stated that all of the Saints then living in Missouri were to leave the state immediately or they would be shot on sight. On November 30, 1838, Joseph Smith and five others were confined in Liberty Jail in Clay County, Missouri. The charges they were held on were of dubious legal merit, but four months later, and after spending the winter in conditions that were primitive at best and criminal at worst, they were still there. They had been mocked and taunted, starved and spat upon. There was precious little in the way of proper bedding or blankets in the single basement cell that held six men, which meant that once the winter cold came it never left, and the ceiling was so low to the ground that Joseph was never able to stand fully erect. Suffice it to say that if such conditions existed today they would immediately be declared cruel and inhumane, and any and all prisoners there would be immediately taken to a safer and more appropriate facility.

But such was not to be the case. During this same period of time the rest of the Saints in Missouri were under constant harassment as directed by the extermination order, and the mobs continued to rape, murder, loot crops, and destroy property.

After four months of what many have called the Prophet's Gethsemane, with nineteen years having passed since the First Vision, after all of the persecutions and betrayals, after all of the stress and pressure associated with the responsibility of his calling as the prophet of the Restoration, finally after all of that—and much, much more—Joseph cried out to God, our Father, with what are some of the most heartbreaking words that we can ever read. He said,

> O God, where art thou? And where is the pavilion that covereth thy hiding place? How long shall thy hand be stayed, and thine eye, yea thy pure eye, behold from the eternal heavens the wrongs of thy people and of thy servants, and thine ear be penetrated with their cries? Yea, O Lord, how long shall they suffer these wrongs and unlawful oppressions, before thine heart shall be softened toward them, and thy bowels be moved with compassion toward them? O Lord God Almighty, maker of heaven, earth, and seas, and of all things that in them are, and who controllest and subjectest the devil, and the dark and benighted dominion of Sheol—stretch forth thy hand; let thine eye pierce; let thy pavilion be taken up; let thy hiding place no longer be covered; let thine ear be inclined; let thine heart be softened, and thy bowels moved with compassion toward us. Let thine anger be kindled against our enemies; and, in the fury of thine heart, with thy sword avenge us of our wrongs. Remember thy suffering saints, O our God; and thy servants will rejoice in thy name forever. (D&C 121:1–6)

Has there ever been, could there ever be, a more plaintive cry than "O God, where art thou? And where is the pavilion that covereth thy hiding place"? If there is, I don't ever want to read or hear it.

But in some very small way I think I can relate to his feelings too. For after almost nine years of our trials, I must admit that there have been a few times that I have felt the desire to pray the same words. I have not done so, however, because I know that the response I would get could only be the same one that Joseph received. Father's response is tender and heartfelt, and it has given me a great sense of peace while also increasing my eternal perspective. His reply is, "My son, peace be unto thy soul; thine adversity and thine afflictions shall be but a small moment; And then, if thou endure it well, God shall exalt thee on high; thou shalt triumph over all thy foes. Thy friends do stand by thee, and they shall hail thee again with warm hears and friendly hands. Thou art not yet as Job; thy friends do not contend against thee, neither charge thee with transgression, as they did Job" (D&C 121:7–10).

And not just my friends, but my wife and children support me too, so what do I have to complain about? For as trying and painful as our circumstances have been and will be, my beloved wife still stands at my side to strengthen me and to help in making me equal to the task at hand, and we still have a reasonable and loving relationship with all four of our children. Could things be better at times? Of course they could. But at the very least we talk regularly, have them in our home for family dinners and time together, and enjoy a comfortable and reasonable association. These are without question the greatest experiences of my life, and I thank God for them on a daily basis. But we are not through with Joseph's experiences yet, for there is much that we can still learn from the insight that he gained from his trials.

The balance of section 121 includes some of the most pointed warnings in all of scripture. There are warnings given to those who would attempt to thwart the work of God, and they are completed with this majestic thought: "How long can rolling waters remain impure? What power shall stay the heavens? As well might man stretch forth his puny arm to stop the Missouri river in its decreed course, or to turn it up stream, as to hinder the Almighty from pouring down knowledge from heaven upon the heads of the Latter-day Saints" (D&C 121:33).

Father then continues on to explain how critical it is that we use the holy priesthood in righteousness and with great understanding and care. Once again, we find some of the greatest words in all of scripture coming to the Prophet during his most desperate hour, but because they do not relate specifically to comforting him during his trials, we will move on without quoting those verses here. You are on your own to review D&C 121:35–46 for the insight and inspiration that they can provide.

Because an expanded eternal perspective and comfort beyond measure is all that is included in section 122, it is quoted here in its entirety. It reads,

> The ends of the earth shall inquire after thy name, and fools shall have thee in derision, and hell shall rage against thee; while the pure in heart, and the wise, and the noble, and the virtuous, shall seek counsel, and authority, and blessing constantly from under thy hand. And thy people shall never be turned against thee by the testimony of traitors. And although their influence shall cast thee into trouble, and into bars and walls, thou shalt be had in honor; and but for a small moment and thy voice shall be more terrible in the midst of thine enemies than the fierce lion, because of thy righteousness; and thy God shall stand by thee forever and ever. (D&C 122:1–4)

So Father begins by explaining to Joseph that the road before him will be very much like the one he has just been on; he then tells him that everything will be all right. He tells him that the priesthood will continue with him, that his trials are but the barest blip on the eternal radar screen, and that based on his continuing righteousness, "God shall stand by thee forever and ever."

These are great words of perspective and comfort for the Prophet, and for us too. But Father is just getting warmed up. He continues,

> If thou art accused with all manner of false accusations; if thine enemies fall upon thee; if they tear thee from the society of thy father and mother and brethren and sisters; and if with a drawn sword thine enemies tear thee from the bosom of thy wife, and of thine offspring, and thine elder son, although but six years of age, shall cling to thy garments, and shall say, My father, my father, why can't you stay with us? O, my father, what are the men going to do with you? and if then he shall be thrust from thee by the sword, and thou be dragged to prison, and thine enemies prowl around thee like wolves for the blood of the lamb; And if thou shouldst be cast into the pit, or into the hands or murderers, and the sentence of death passed upon thee; if thou be cast into the deep; if the billowing surge conspire against thee; if fierce winds become thine enemy; if the heavens gather blackness, and all the elements combine to hedge up the way; and above all, if the very jaws of hell shall gape open the mouth wide after thee. (D&C 122:6–7)

Some comfort, right? If that's a helpful eternal perspective, you say, I'd rather not, thank you very much. With a list as awful as that one, you might even think that Father is trying to depress Joseph and break his spirit. After all, how could it get any worse than "if the very jaws of hell shall gape open the mouth wide after thee"? But unless you finish reading verse 7—in the same way that you need to see your own trials through to the end—you will never gain the understanding that Father has in store for you. For here is the payoff, here is understanding and perspective that stretches from one side of an infinite and unending universe to the other. Father finishes by saying, "Know thou, my son, that *all these things shall give thee experience, and shall be for thy good*" (D&C 121:7; italics added).

I don't know about any of you, but for me, if Joseph had stopped there it would have been enough. For this is enough perspective; this is enough love; there is enough that is good and holy in these few words that it would have been enough if he had stopped there. And if he had been but a normal man he would have. But in one of the greatest examples of his prophetic calling that we can ever have, Joseph continued writing because Father was not yet finished teaching us about what really matters.

He continues, "The Son of Man hath descended below them all. *Art thou greater than he?*" (D&C 122:8; italics added). Thus, with the same kind of certainty created by the spikes in the Savior's hands, wrists, and feet; with the same ability as the spear to pierce to the very heart of the matter; Father focuses our hearts, souls, and minds on the one being who is "mighty to save" (2 Nephi 19:31). He points us to the only real source of healing, mercy, peace, and comfort. He simply and eloquently gives us the perspective and comfort that we need so desperately, and in doing so he refers us to the one who said, "Come unto me, all ye that labour and are heavy laden, and I will give you rest" (Matthew 11:28).

Isn't it ironic that a simple bumper sticker is able to teach these most magnificent of all truths in eight simple words:

No Christ, No Peace
Know Christ, Know Peace

So when the inevitable challenges come—either through others' choices or your own—are you still going to try to claim that no one else can understand? Please, I beg of you, do not fall back on such shallow and limited thinking. For I truly believe the scripture that states,

> Jesus, who was made a little lower than the angels for the suffering of death, crowned with glory and honour; that he by the grace of God should taste death for every man. For it became him, for whom are all

> things, and by whom are all things, in bringing many sons unto glory, to make the captain of their salvation perfect through sufferings. For both he that sanctifieth and they who are sanctified are all of one: for which cause he is not ashamed to call them brethren, Saying, I will declare thy name unto my brethren, in the midst of the church will I sing praise unto thee. And again, I will put my trust in him. And again, Behold I and the children which God hath given me. Forasmuch then as the children are partakers of flesh and blood, he also himself likewise took part of the same; that through death he might destroy him that had the power of death, that is, the devil; And deliver them who through fear of death were all their lifetime subject to bondage. For verily he took not on him the nature of angels; but he took on him the seed of Abraham. Wherefore in all things it behoved him to be made like unto his brethren, that he might be a merciful and faithful high priest in things pertaining to God, to make reconciliation for the sins of the people. For in that he himself hath suffered being tempted, he is able to succor them that are tempted. (Hebrews 2:9–18)

Later we read, "He that ascended up on high, as also he descended below *all* things, in that he comprehended *all* things, that he might be in all and through all things, the light of truth" (D&C 88:6; italics added). And so we could continue, ad infinitum and to worlds without end. But you have your own copy of the scriptures, and you can find all of those additional references just as easily as I can. So let's move on.

Notes

1. Boyd K. Packer, "Our Moral Environment," Ensign, May 1992; italics added.
2. Ibid.

6.7 To Swim in Deep Water or to Climb Mountains?

ON SEPTEMBER 1, 1842, JUST A LITTLE OVER A YEAR AND a half before his martyrdom, Joseph wrote the following as part of a revelation concerning the work of baptizing for the dead. He said, "Nevertheless, deep water is what I am wont to swim in. It all has become a second nature to me; and I feel, like Paul, to glory in tribulation; for to this day has the God of my fathers delivered me out of them all, and will deliver me from henceforth; for behold, and lo, I shall triumph over all my enemies, for the Lord God hath spoken it" (D&C 127:2). I may not know the feeling as well as he did, but I can at least identify with the sentiment.

For I too glory in the challenges. Through it all I have continued to ask the twin questions, "What can I learn from all of this?" and "What does Father want me to learn from this?" I am also eternally indebted to him for his tender and loving support and the council that he has so willingly bestowed on me, and though the path has been far from easy, I can honestly say that I am grateful for all that I have learned.

It is also my responsibility to add my humble testimony to all those who have gone before by declaring my personal witness of the divinity of Jesus Christ and his life and sacrifice on my behalf. This is something that—because of my many faults, shortcomings, transgressions, and sins—I take very personally. I have to, for it has been plainly manifest to me that unless he is willing to stand at my side and say to God, our Father, "I know this one doesn't look like much, and we all three know how far he is from perfect, but his heart is truly broken and his spirit is contrite, so that makes him acceptable to me," I am forever lost and without hope, and there would be no reason to continue the battle.

But such is not the case, for I know to the depths of my soul that Jesus is the Christ and the son of Almighty God. I know that he was resurrected on the third day, and that he lives and rules at his Father's side as the Savior and Redeemer of the world. He is my strength and my salvation and the only source to which I can turn to heal my soul and find the peace and comfort that are so desperately needed if I am to continue to deal with the challenges that are placed before me. I further know that through the power of the holy priesthood and the sealing covenant, if my dear wife and I do the best we can, if we keep the covenants that we made at a holy altar, our posterity will yet be afforded opportunities to accept Jesus Christ that are beyond our imaginings, and that those opportunities can still allow them to gain their "eternal exaltation in spite of earth and hell."[1] I pray with all of my heart that the things contained here will assist you in your attempt to do the same.

But, unlike Joseph, I'm not much of a swimmer, so here is the best I can come up with as a personal analogy to finish up.

It is now Christmas 2006, and it's been almost three months since I went for my last bike ride. Between the ongoing treatment program with our child and my writing efforts, my focus has been on other things for a while. It's the dead of winter, our high temperatures have been below freezing for the past week, and since I absolutely hate riding indoors, my physical activity is currently limited to building some strength with body weight exercises and some minor cardio efforts.

Now don't get me wrong, I take about a six-week semi-break from serious training every fall, but at my age it takes so long to get the strength back that I can never stop completely, I simply have to keep going throughout the winter. If I don't, it takes the entire summer just to get back to where I was the previous fall, and I really hate that feeling. So I keep at it. I keep plugging away with my core building exercises, and I do lots of different things to build strength and endurance in my legs and lower body.

Why, you ask? Why put so much work and effort into something as trivial as riding a bicycle? For the very same reasons that I keep working on my spirituality and on my relationship with God, our Father, and his precious Son, Jesus Christ.

Because I love the challenge of it all.

Because I know that I can always improve.

Because while I may not know what is coming in my personal life, I know for sure that spring is coming, and there will always be another mountain to climb.

Notes

1. Brigham Young, in *Journal of Discourses* (London: Latter-day Saints' Book Depot, 1854–86), 2:31.

About the Author

ALAN WAS BORN AND RAISED IN THE SALT LAKE CITY area, and after graduating from high school he served a full-time mission in the Arizona Tempe Mission from 1975 to 1977. His twenty-five-year professional life has been in the sales field.

His Church service has included serving as a counselor in the bishopric, stake high counselor, stake Young Men president, and teaching Gospel Doctrine, Gospel Essentials, and the high priests group. He currently serves as the teachers quorum advisor in his ward.

Alan's hobbies include acting in semi-professional and community theatre productions in the Salt Lake City area, and riding a bicycle between twenty-five hundred and three thousand miles a year.

As this book goes to press, he and his wife, Linda, will celebrate twenty-nine years of marriage. They are the parents of four children and one grandchild.

This is his first book.

0 26575 70954 4